I0759829

ANGLISTISCHE FORSCHUNGEN
Band 437

Begründet von
Johannes Hoops

Herausgegeben von
Rüdiger Ahrens
Heinz Antor
Klaus Stierstorfer

BARBARA KORTE
FRÉDÉRIC REGARD (Eds.)

Narrating "Precariousness"

Modes, Media, Ethics

Universitätsverlag
WINTER
Heidelberg

Bibliografische Information der Deutschen Nationalbibliothek
Die Deutsche Nationalbibliothek verzeichnet diese Publikation in der Deutschen Nationalbibliografie; detaillierte bibliografische Daten sind im Internet über *http://dnb.d-nb.de* abrufbar.

Ouvrage publié avec le concours de l'Université Paris-Sorbonne

ISBN 978-3-8253-6213-3

Imprimé en Allemagne · Printed in Germany
Druck: Memminger MedienCentrum, 87700 Memmingen

Gedruckt auf umweltfreundlichem, chlorfrei gebleichtem und alterungsbeständigem Papier

Den Verlag erreichen Sie im Internet unter:
www.winter-verlag.de

Table of Contents

Barbara Korte and Frédéric Regard

Narrating 'Precariousness': Modes, Media and Ethics[1]

1. Introduction

The interest of this book in 'precariousness' is embedded in the revival of humanist criticism and the 'ethical turn'.[2] Such criticism focuses its attention on moral issues and on moral response, and it is unsurprising that it often centres on the 'bareness'[3] and fragility of human life, as well as the perils and misery to which it can be exposed. The contributions to our book also focus on the portrayal of lives that are 'precarious': insecure, unpredictable, endangered, on the edge and out of balance, threatened in their corporeal and mental integrity, and therefore often resulting in trauma.[4] Such lives call to mind the relationality of human existence and demand intersubjective recognition such as sympathy, empathy[5] and the "basic social emotion" of compassion (Nussbaum),[6] while they also often invite more dubious reactions such as a voyeuristic gaze and vicarious pleasure. But such lives do not only pose an ethical challenge – they are just as often a challenge to representation. A leading question of this volume is therefore how precarious and injured lives can be represented – and thus become recognisable – even when their circumstances seem unspeakable in both the literal and the metaphorical sense.

At the present cultural moment, much attention is awarded to the precarity caused by re-organisations of the labour market, the globalisation of neoliberal capitalism and the recent wave of inequality and poverty it has generated worldwide.[7] But life is also rendered precarious by many other causes: the devastations caused by war and terror, the (ab-)use of science and technology, exploitation of the environment, political perse-

1 For their invaluable help in getting this volume ready for publication, we would like to thank Katja Bay, Natalie Churn and Kathrin Göb.

2 The objectives of the ethical turn in literary studies are "issues of how humans live and what they live for", and this presupposes that representations bear a relation to pre-representational worlds and communicate values that matter to their producers and consumers (Schwarz 3).

3 On the notion of bare life as "life exposed to death" and thus representing "the originary political element" cf. Agamben (88).

4 For a definition of trauma cf., for instance, Cathy Caruth: "an overwhelming experience of sudden or catastrophic events in which the response to the event occurs in the often delayed, uncontrolled repetitive appearance of hallucinations and other intrusive phenomena" (11).

5 On empathy vs. sympathy (as instant identification) cf. Richard Sennett's *Together*.

6 Cf. Berlant's *Compassion* for a critical discussion of compassion which, as a claim for ameliorative action, can also entail ethically dubious practices such as the measuring of dif-ferent scales of suffering.

7 On cultural representations of poverty cf. Korte and Regard, and Korte and Zipp.

cution, voluntary and enforced migration, sexual exploitation, or racial and gender discrimination. Apart from pre-individual causes, there is also, of course, the distress people face individually, for instance when afflicted with serious illness or personal loss and deprivation. Reasons to investigate the dangers to human life are manifold and many-faceted, and the chapters of this book illustrate this range. They also, however, take issue with the ways in which critics and theorists have conceived 'precariousness'.

Since Butler's seminal *Precarious Life* (2004), the terms 'precarious' and 'precariousness' have proliferated in scholarly debate with various shades of meaning and not always as clearly defined terms. It is therefore an aim of this volume to explore the analytical reach and power of these concepts – not primarily through abstract discussion, however, but through case studies of ways in which precarious *lives* have been represented in various modes and media. The focus of these studies is on narrative representation because, as Todd Davis and Kenneth Womack claim, "[pa]rt of being human involves the daily struggle with the meanings and consequences of our actions", and this struggle is "most often understood in narrative structures as we tell others and ourselves about what has transpired or what we fear will transpire in the future" (ix). The "act of telling stories", understood as "the gesture to represent what all too often is unrepresentable, ineffable", is one that "grounds and distinguishes human activity" (ix-x). Some chapters critique Butler explicitly and replace or complement her categories with concepts from a range of other disciplines, including psychoanalysis and trauma studies as well as ecocriticism. Most importantly, all chapters concretise 'precariousness' through the lens of cultural production as they investigate novels, films, photo books, theatre plays, poetry, hip-hop, graphic novels and computer games. In *The Weight of the World*, Pierre Bourdieu emphasises the importance of literature's particularity and complexity for the representation of 'miserable' lives, and recommends the novel as a model for sociologists: "following the lead of novelists such as Faulkner, Joyce or Woolf, we must relinquish the single, central, dominant, in a word, quasi-divine, point of view that is all too easily adopted by observers – and by readers too, at least to the extent they do not feel personally involved" (3). The case studies in the present book treat literature, film and other representations in similar ways: as manifestations of real and fictional situations and figures that are particular rather than general and thus permit the testing of Butler's and other thinkers' categories for ethical-cultural analysis.

2. 'Precarious Life' Revisited

For Butler, 'precariousness' is originally a category – which she further elaborates in later writings such as *Frames of War* (2009) and her 2011 Neale Wheeler Watson lecture – to grasp a fundamental, ontological fragility of corporeal existence that is common to all living beings. As she states in her preface to the essays in *Precarious Life*, they were written "in response to the conditions of heightened vulnerability and aggression" that followed the events of 9/11 (xi). When this terrible toll on human life was taken, she writes, "an unbearable vulnerability was exposed" (xi), and she takes "injurability and aggression" (xii) as points of departure for her new conception of political life. According to Butler, the Twin Towers events force us to think of political life as an "inevitable interdependency" (xii) – an interdependency she finds difficult to theorise, as she finally confesses (xiii). In part, this difficulty may be connected with some imprecisions in Butler's use of terms: in her 2004 *Precarious Life*, the adjective 'precarious' refers to both precariousness as a general property of life *and* a more concrete precarity – in the sense of an insecure existence and a higher probability of experiencing suffering – that is *not* equally distributed (and therefore poses an ethical challenge): "There are ways of distributing vulnerability, differential forms of allocation that make some populations more subject to arbitrary violence than others" (xii). The word 'precarity', however, is not used in the 2004 publication.[8] Just as importantly, Butler tends to conflate the terms 'precariousness' and 'vulnerability', sometimes using them interchangeably even though their etymology reveals different structural assumptions behind them. The adjective 'vulnerable' comes from the Latin verb 'vul-nerare': to wound, to injure, to offend. The verb itself comes from the noun 'vulnus', which means a wound, an injury, a cut, but also a pain, a blow, a twist of fate. The *OED* comes to the conclusion that a vulnerable being is susceptible to being wounded, either physically or psychologically. 'Vulnerability' forces me to acknowledge the presence of another who can hurt me, which implies a power relationship. Self and other are caught in a structure of violent *opposition between an offender and an offended*. 'Precariousness' comes from the Latin adjective 'precarius': "given as a favour, depending on the favour of another". Its meaning is derived from the verb 'precor', which means to pray, or to supplicate, and it survived in a now obsolete definition of the English 'precarious' with the meaning "suppliant, supplicating; importunate". The *OED* illustrates this notion by quoting from an article written by Dr Johnson in 1753: a precarious being, he explains, is a being "incessantly solliciting [sic] the assistance of others". The *OED* adds that what may be said of a human being may also be said of an argument which would be insufficiently grounded and therefore liable to fail. Precariousness may therefore be said to define a being or a statement which would be dependent on chance and circumstance, *dependent*, that is, *on the good will or on the pleasure of the other*. Butler's discussion of precariousness, which is strongly centred on the perception and recognition of an

[8] In *Frames of War*, Butler distinguishes between precariousness and precarity: 'precariousness' is here defined as a *social*-ontological category that "implies living socially, that is, the fact that one's life is always in some sense in the hands of the other" (14), while 'precarity' is "that politically induced condition in which certain populations suffer from failing social and economic networks of support and become differentially exposed to injury, violence, and death. Such populations are at heightened risk of disease, poverty, starvation, displacement, and of exposure to violence without protection. Precarity also characterizes that politically induced condition of maximized precariousness for populations exposed to arbitrary state violence who often have no other option than to appeal to the very state from which they need protection" (26). Butler's use of terms has particularly attracted criticism in the context of labour. Neilson and Rossiter, for instance, suggest that precariousness as an ontological and existential category should be distinguished more clearly "from precarity intended in the labour market sense", where the term "refers to all possible shapes of unsure, not guaranteed, flexible exploitation", but also "extends beyond the world of work to encompass other aspects of intersubjective life, including housing, debt, and the ability to build affective social relations". For a critical discussion of Butler's terms from the perspective of governance studies cf. Lorey.

other's precarious life,[9] tends to neglect the pragmatic dimension that Johnson's use still entails: that precariousness forces me to acknowledge the *presence of an other as an addressee*, someone who may, or may not, listen to my calls for help. Again, this is a different structure than in the case of vulnerability. First, it is no longer a structure of violent opposition, implying an asymmetrical power relationship. Rather, it is a structure of communication, implying a dialogical relationship. Interdependency is also linguistic, and it implies an enunciative setup. Second, it is no longer a purely binary structure involving two antagonistic agencies – an offender and an offended. The structure accommodates the possibility of a third source of agency, a third actant on the scene of interdependency – a witness if you like, or a writer, journalist, novelist, dramatist, who may or may not acknowledge the existence, or the importance of the plight, of the vulnerable person. This third agent is the one who may redistribute positions and redefine the offender as criminal and the offended as victim.

It is precisely this third agency through which this volume approaches precariousness and its political and moral implications. As Susan Sontag has poignantly argued in *Regarding the Pain of Others*, human suffering calls for engaged attention and reaction when it is witnessed and when it is represented,[10] and in a side remark she claims that narrative representation may be "more effective than an image" in this respect, partly because of the length of time a narrative obliges one to look and to feel (122). All our contributors provide close readings of the essentially narrative representations they scrutinise. As will thus become evident, not only are the lives represented in these texts precarious in multiple ways, but in many instances the very means of representation themselves become precarious as they struggle to express what seems to evade or even explode the sense-making mechanisms of narration. It may be useful here to once more go back to the etymology of the word 'precarious' as "obtained by entreaty, depending on the favour of another". In order to be represented, precarious and injured lives often depend on the 'favour' of people who do not live precariously themselves. Hence the question of agency over representation (as famously raised by Gayatri Spivak) and specifically of the kinds of "voice" or "embodied position" (Couldry 8) through which precariousness is articulated or mediated. As Nick Couldry reminds us, voice in this sense is a basic human value: it "values my and your status as 'narratable' selves" (13) and "involves, from the start, both speaking and *listening*, that is, an act of attention that registers the uniqueness of the other's narrative" (8). If those who narrate precarious

[9] Especially in her discussion of Levinas in her 2004 publication. Here Butler posits that precarious life implies a particular "structure of address" (130), and that this structure is at the core of the Levinasian notion of 'face': "To respond to the face, to understand its meaning, means to be awake to what is precarious in another life, or, rather, the precariousness of life itself. This cannot be an awakeness [...] to my own life, and then an extrapolation from an understanding of my own precariousness to an understanding of another's precarious life. It has to be an understanding of the precariousness of the Other. This is what makes the face belong to the sphere of ethics" (134).

[10] Compare this to Slavoj Žižek's reflections on subjective and systemic violence and his position that violence should be thought through not from an engaged but a distanced position: "There are situations when the only truly 'practical' thing to do is to resist the temptation to engage immediately and to 'wait and see' by means of a patient, critical analysis. Engagement seems to exert its pressure on us from all directions" (6).

lives have an ethical obligation, so have the addressees of these narratives. Our chapters attest to the basic 'narratability' of precarious existence, while being sensitive to the potentials and limitations of this narratability in different modes and media.

3. The Case Studies

The cases discussed in our chapters range across the anglophone world, but a focus on the late twentieth and early twenty-first centuries allows for an analysis of the cultural moment that inspired Butler's and other thinkers' ethical inquiry. Beyond their special concerns, the chapters together address general questions implicated in narrations of precarious lives. How are ethical positions negotiated in the interplay between the represented on the one hand and agents of representation on the other? How do narratives cope with the seeming ineffability of precarious and injured lives? How do different media and genres, or narrative agencies and strategies, configure precariousness differently? How do narrative representations 'perform' precariousness? How can representation inspire the social imagination, evoke social emotions and configure possibilities of action?

The case studies are grouped into two major areas: precarious worlds and precarious selves. In the first section, Lena Steveker looks at fictional re-evaluations of the two world wars which determined European and world politics throughout the twentieth century. Pat Barker's *Regeneration* trilogy is engaged with demythologising the 'Great' War, while A. L. Kennedy's *Day* is concerned with undermining the notion of the Second World War as a 'just' one which the British fought in defence of civilisation and humanity. Each author's fiction problematises the damaging effects which the inhumane conditions of industrial warfare have on human psychic stability. Both Barker's trilogy and Kennedy's novel feature protagonists whose traumatic war experiences have caused them to develop split personalities; and it is with the help of these characters' mental instabilities that the texts negotiate the precarious consequences entailed in a self's complete loss of control and power over one's own well-being. But while Kennedy's *Day* is indebted to liberal humanism in its celebration of 'high' art and its supposed unifying effects on human selfhood, Barker's novels suggest a reconciliation of traumatised self and internal other which is best analysed through the lens of Levinasian ethics: her trilogy privileges a concept of dual, if not multiple selfhood by representing healing as the ethical acceptance of difference, not its repression or expulsion. Thus, Barker's novels defy the violence which, according to Levinas, comes from subjecting the other to the self's understanding.

Barbara Kowalczuk discusses photography of the Vietnam War by the Welsh photographer Philip Jones Griffiths, who covered the war for the Magnum photo agency. His three-year-long work was printed in *Vietnam Inc.* (1971), which was immediately recognised as a landmark in concerned photojournalism. For more than three decades, Griffiths returned to Vietnam to capture postwar life and he eventually published two other major books, *Agent Orange: Collateral Damage in Viet Nam* and *Viet Nam at Peace*. Drawing on Susan Sontag's seminal work on photography, Kowalczuk claims that this trilogy's narrative thread apprehends the essence of precariousness through a restricted selection of photographs which establish a network of gazes. Her discussion focuses on a paradigm which, from eye-to-eye confrontations to upsetting blank looks, reveals that the photographic chronicles of the Vietnam Trilogy are themselves precarious as they generate inconclusive, not to say perilous, narrative hermeneutics.

Rudolph Glitz turns to a motif repeatedly occurring in popular science fiction: the figure of the feral child that challenges notions of humanism and a civilised society. Glitz discusses two films, George Miller's *The Road Warrior* (1981) from the *Mad Max* series and James Cameron's *Aliens* (1986), as well as the more recent computer game *BioShock* (2007). In all three narratives, the protagonists with whom recipients are encouraged to identify encounter the precarious human other in the form of a feral child of some sort, whose vulnerable and simultaneously threatening characteristics recall Levinas's notion of the face as invoked and endorsed by Butler. Glitz scrutinises the political and moral implications of the three narratives and shows how they can be related to debates about the condition of precariousness and possibilities of its representation. Glitz reads the three science-fiction narratives through pertinent sections of Butler's *Precarious Life* (2004) and Lee Edelman's contribution to queer studies, *No Future* (2004), and then shows how the narratives challenge Edelman's and Butler's arguments.

The power of popular media to address the ethical challenges of precarious lives is also demonstrated by Gabriele Rippl and Stephanie Hoppeler, who turn to another popular medium. Graphic novels and comic books are an intermedial form of storytelling that often engages with devastating experiences such as war and terror, totalitarianism and the Holocaust as well as domestic and individual forms of violence and trauma. Hoppeler and Rippl investigate how graphic novels and comic books published since the 1960s have treated the scientific, medical and military use of radioactivity and its consequences for human life: as a daunting apocalypse which leads to excruciating experiences, but also as an exciting negotiation of limits. Since scenarios such as nuclear disaster challenge conventional language and commonsense reasoning, their representation is itself precarious. Rippl and Hoppeler show how graphic novels and comic books with their intermedial narration have a special potential to enhance their readers' participation and to express trauma, fears and anxieties through pictures and visual codes in ways that are precluded in purely verbal narratives.

Ellen Dengel-Janic identifies 'precarious geographies' in the novels of Amitav Ghosh. In his works, the Indian author portrays a multitude of characters that are affected by the precariousness caused by migration and diasporic experience, thereby creating a variety of 'cartographic narratives' in the sense of J. Edward Mallot. While the main focus of Ghosh's early novel *The Shadow Lines* (1988) lies in the impact of history *on* geographical locations, the precariousness of nature moves centre stage in *The Hungry Tide* (2005). In his first outright ecocritical novel, Ghosh intertwines the precarious social position of his characters with their perilous and shifting regional location in the tide country of the Ganges delta.

The second section is dedicated to representations of precarious selves. Stephan Laqué discusses Mike Leigh's feature film *Naked* (1993) as a pronounced break with other films by Leigh which tend to follow a pattern of benign, suburban middle-class characters bravely shouldering their damaged lives. *Naked* departs from this pattern not only in subject matter and character, but also in technique: if Leigh's films are commonly concerned with economic and social precarity, *Naked* addresses more fundamental questions of precariousness, namely of unstable subject formations and forms of existence. Laqué argues that Johnny, the film's protagonist, is a study in the extremes to which human 'nakedness' in the sense of self-exposure can be pushed. He is created as a cynic in the Foucauldian sense: as a person who embraces *parrhesia*, the compulsion to say everything, to speak the truth regardless of the consequences. His *parrhesia* is postmodern both in that it playfully subverts other people's faith in certainty and coherence, and in that it is entirely fuelled by language, by Johnny's incessant rhetorical bravado and competitiveness rather than by the ethical agenda which motivates classical cynics. Being "naked" – on the street and without a job – is as much part of Johnny's 'care of himself' (Foucault) as his rhetorical self-exposure. His tangible immorality keeps our attitude towards the character suspended between admiration and contempt, between empathy and revulsion – a suitably precarious response to a magnificent exploration of the radical precariousness which contemporary cynicism entails.

Jagna Oltarzewska explores the rapper Eminem's autofictions. Eminem's progress, from his early album *The Slim Shady LP* (1999), has been punctuated by a series of 'reality' songs that chronicle the experience of his coming-of-age in a violent and poverty-stricken milieu and his rise to superstardom with its ambivalent rewards. These involve an elaborate and unsparing self-staging: Eminem's troubled family history, his dysfunctional relationships with family members, the pressures of fame, his struggle with depression, drug-addiction, and his spell in rehab and consequent recovery have all been grist to the mill. The precarious life that Eminem references is that of a trashed and disposable population, and his lyrics embrace the African-American experience as much as his own, as a token white practitioner of rap whose skills were honed on the black hip hop circuits of Detroit. His narratives mirror the adversarial milieu and harsh experiences he has known, and are openly provocative. Obscenity imparts its own species of precarious life to the rapper's narrative content, threatening to overpower it, and raising inevitable questions concerning the possibility of (self-)representation. Oltarzewska brings the concept of "linguistic conjuncture", as elaborated by Jean-Jacques Lecercle, to bear on the seam of obscenity tapped by Eminem (and other 'reality' rappers); it forces the listener to situate extreme verbal provocation within a complex, evolving set of discourses 'con-joined' to the economic and political, directing attention to a linguistic moment which illuminates the emergence and current vitality of inflammatory speech.

Marc Amfreville's chapter gives a reading of Sapphire's *Push* (1996) with reference to what Butler, in her 2011 Neale Wheeler Watson lecture, refers to as "the obligation of proximity". She thus raises the question of the ethical necessity for a closeness to precariousness, while also advocating an indispensable distance from the subject of our concern: empathy rather than sympathy. Amfreville asks how *Push* manages to plunge its reader into the mind of a sixteen-year old victim of incest, while maintaining a non-voyeuristic stance. To Amfreville, the answer lies in the very act and form of narration. *Push*, for all its apparently spontaneous, candid, often obscene appearances, is a carefully wrought narrative, informed by the recognition and staging of various mechanisms that make it a telling example of how literature can transcend its own documentary value to achieve aesthetic and ethical relevance. Amfreville draws his theoretical input from the theory of trauma, and more precisely from Freud's early and little-read "Project for a Scientific Psychology" (1895), intending to show how Sapphire's book stages utter precariousness in such a way that it takes us to the core of the issue of representation, the Freudian concepts being used not to describe the character's "case", but serving to probe into the very functioning of the text itself. Amfreville first deals with "*Bahnung*" (facilitation), the way in which a second or third trauma is made easier by the existence of one or several former traumas in the history of the subject. He then deals with narration as a healing process, resorting to the concept of "*Nebenmensch*" or fellow being, and finally, going back to Butler's interrogations, reintroduces the concept of "*Hilflosigkeit*" (helplessness) as a hallmark of the protagonist's precarious life, but above all the spring of empathy.

Hélène Aji reads Lyn Hejinian's poems as texts that struggle between determinacy and the anxiety of indeterminacy, between closure and the rejection of closure, between ideology and the debunking of ideological discourse. By questioning the very form of expression in language, this major member of the American Language Poets elaborates alternate modes of expression that eschew the sentimentality of self-expression. She has also been foregrounding the tension between the delusions of stability and rationality constructed by conventional discourses expressed in the forms of conventional syntax, and the intrinsic precariousness of actual living. By reactivating the etymology of "happy" in a number of her writings, Hejinian inscribes precariousness in the very human condition, as a plight to be lived with, and not against. Indeed, by going back to the etymology of the adverb "happily" in her choice of the title to the poem that follows her recovery from cancer, she underscores the relief of survival, which inexorably mingles with the sentiment of pointlessness and chance. Happiness is what happens in unfathomable ways that belie the commonplace optimism of the term. The poetic enterprise consequently turns into an obstinate and endless process of rationalisation, not through the production of linear, smooth, reassuring narratives that would offer a shelter from the randomness of fate, but through the streamlining of discourse in procedural texts that iteratively undertake to integrate the lacunae and discrepancies of partial, selective, inventive memories.

Elisabeth Angel-Perez addresses the representation of precarious life in theatre with a strong narrative impulse. It is Angel-Perez's contention that the paradox of the plays she investigates is that they spectralise the body as if to make it clear that the more visually absent the onstage body, the more present its suffering; the more hidden the body, the more real its precariousness. To lose sight, in the theatre, would therefore not be a tragedy any more, but on the contrary, could well be the guarantee of an *ontos*: only the 'not-being-seen' on the stage would allow us to have access to the thing as it is. This chapter analyses the advent of this new (post-)phenomenological aesthetics by exploring how playwrights such as Sarah Kane, Martin Crimp or debbie tucker green have decided to poeticise precariousness on the stage, therefore compelling the spectator to renegotiate the visual contract.

Works Cited

Agamben, Giorgio. *Homo Sacer: Sovereign Power and Bare Life*. Stanford, CA: Stanford University Press, 1998.

Berlant, Lauren, ed. *Compassion: The Culture and Politics of an Emotion*. New York and London: Routledge, 2004.

Bourdieu, Pierre, ed. *The Weight of the World: Social Suffering in Contemporary Society*. Stanford, CA: Stanford University Press, 1999. [*La Misère du monde*. Paris: Seuil, 1993].

Butler, Judith. *Precarious Life: The Powers of Mourning and Violence*. London: Verso, 2004.

Butler, Judith. *Frames of War: When Life is Grievable?* New York and London: Verso, 2009.

Butler, Judith. "Precarious Life: The Obligations of Proximity." Neale Wheeler Watson Lecture. *The European Graduate School*. 24 May 2011. Retrieved 23 Sep. 2013. <http://www.egs.edu/faculty/judith-butler/videos/precarious-life-the-obligations-of-proximity/>.

Caruth, Cathy. *Unclaimed Experience: Trauma, Narrative and History*. Baltimore, MD: Johns Hopkins University Press, 1996.

Couldry, Nick. *Why Voice Matters: Culture and Politics after Neoliberalism*. London: Sage, 2010.

Davis, Todd F. and Kenneth Womack, eds. "Preface: Reading Literature and the Ethics of Criticism." *Mapping the Ethical Turn: A Reader in Ethics, Culture and Literary Theory*. Charlottesville: University Press of Virginia, 2001. ix-xiv.

Korte, Barbara and Frederic Regard, eds. *Narrating Poverty and Precarity in Britain: Literary and Cultural Perspectives*. [Forthcoming.]

Korte, Barbara and Georg Zipp. *Poverty in Contemporary Literature: Themes and Figurations on the British Book Market*. London: Palgrave Pivot, 2014.

Lorey, Isabell. 2011. "Governmental Precarization." *European Institute for Progressive Cultural Policies*. January 2011. Retrieved 25 September 2013. <http://eipcp.net/transversal/0811/lorey/en>.

Neilson, Brett, and Ned Rossiter, "From Precarity to Precariousness and Back Again: Labour, Life and Unstable Networks." *The Fibreculture Journal* 5 (2005). Retrieved 20 Oct. 2013. <http://five.Fibreculturejournal.org/fcj-022-from-precarity-to-precariousness-and-back-again-labour-life-and-unstable-networks/>.

Nussbaum, Martha. "Compassion: The Basic Social Emotion." *Social Philosophy and Policy* 13 (1996): 27-38.

"precariousness, n." *The Oxford English Dictionary*. Online edition 2013. Retrieved 20 Oct. 2013. <http://www.oed.com/view/Entry/149550?redirectedFrom=Precariousness#eid>.

Schwarz, Daniel R. "A Humanistic Ethics of Reading." *Mapping the Ethical Turn: A Reader in Ethics, Culture and Literary Theory*. Ed. Todd F. Davis and Kenneth Womack. Charlottesville: University Press of Virginia, 2001. 3-15.

Sennett, Richard. *Together: The Rituals, Pleasures and Politics of Cooperation*. New Haven, CT: Yale University Press, 2012.

Sontag, Susan. *Regarding the Pain of Others*. New York: Farrar, Straus and Giroux, 2003.

Spivak, Gayatri Chakravorty. "Can the Subaltern Speak?" *Marxism and the Interpretation of Culture*. Ed. Cary Nelson and Lawrence Grossberg. Urbana: University of Illinois Press, 1988. 271-313.

"vulnerable, adj." *The Oxford English Dictionary*. Online edition 2013. Retrieved 20 Oct. 2013. <http://www.oed.com/view/Entry/224872?redirectedFrom=vulnerable#eid>.

Žižek, Slavoj. *Violence: Six Sideways Reflections*. 2008. London: Profile Books, 2009.

Part One

Precarious Worlds

Lena Steveker

Precarious Selves in Contemporary British War Novels

> [T]hat an unbearable vulnerability was exposed, that a terrible toll on human life was taken, were, and are, cause for fear and for mourning. [...]
> That we can be injured, that others can be injured, that we are subject to death at the whim of another, are all reasons for both fear and grief (Butler xi-xii).

I

World Wars One and Two are the two military conflicts which feature most prominently in contemporary British war novels. Although more recent wars such as those fought in Iraq and Afghanistan as well as the so-called 'war on terror' have found entry into British fiction,[1] the majority of war novels published in the last two decades revolve around either one of the two wars which have had lasting influence on twentieth-century politics and cultures in Britain, Europe and the world. Texts such as Pat Barker's *Regeneration* trilogy as well as her novels *Another World* (1998), *Life Class* (2007) and *Toby's Room* (2012), Ian McEwan's *Atonement* (2001), Sebastian Faulks's *Birdsong* (2003), Sarah Waters' *The Night Watch* (2006), A. L. Kennedy's *Day* (2007) and Louisa Young's *My Dear, I Wanted to Tell You* (2011) testify to the central position these two wars still hold in British war fiction.[2] Novels such as those listed above represent war through the lens of personal experience and individual suffering. Thus, they tap into a literary tradition first established by the trench poets of the First World War whose texts negotiate the horrors of industrialized warfare by focussing on individual soldiers' ordeals, their pain and death.[3] To this strategy of personalization contemporary British war novels add a strategy of internalization, thus foregrounding the disastrous effects the characters' war experiences have on their minds and their mental stability.

[1] For example, novels such as Pat Barker's *Double Vision* (2003), Ian McEwan's *Saturday* (2005) and Chris Cleave's *Incendiary* (2005) centre on these wars.

[2] For a list of contemporary British novels published before 2002 discussing other British wars cf. Korte and Schneider (1).

[3] In contrast to the trench poetry, war memoirs and novels published during the First World War and its aftermath, preceding literary renderings of war rely on strategies of depersonalization. British poetry of the Crimean war, for instance, typically "portrays a global view of the general mayhem but does not show individual suffering. [...] The unbearable cruelty of war is thus depersonalized, and the readers of poetry are spared the gruesome details" (Rommel 113).

These strategies are especially pronounced in Pat Barker's *Regeneration* trilogy and A.L. Kennedy's novel *Day*, which I will discuss in the following. Both authors' novels tell stories of soldiers' sufferings caused by their experiences during the First World War and the Second World War, respectively. Set in 1917 and 1918, Barker's three novels *Regeneration* (1991), *The Eye in the Door* (1993) and *Ghost Road* (1995)[4] focus on British soldiers sent back to Britain for treatment of the post-traumatic stress disorders they developed whilst serving in the trenches on the Western Front. Suffering from various forms of what was once described as 'shell-shock',[5] Barker's characters, most prominent among them an officer called Billy Prior, struggle to cope with the atrocities they have been forced to experience in this first fully industrialized war. When the reader first meets Prior in *Regeneration*, the officer is a patient at Craiglockhart War Hospital where he has been sent to suffering from nightmares, amnesia, and mutism (*Regeneration* 38). After he has regained both his memory and his voice with the help of the psychiatrist and medical officer Dr Rivers, Prior discovers in *The Eye in the Door* that he has also developed a split personality. Having been able to "heal the split" (*Eye* 402), Prior has himself declared fit for service and, in *The Ghost Road*, returns to France where he dies in a British attack on the German lines only days before the war is over.

It is the condition of dissociation which Barker's Billy Prior shares with the eponymous protagonist of Kennedy's novel *Day*. The novel is set in 1949 when former RAF tail-gunner Alfred Day returns to Germany as an extra to a film project about a prisoner-of-war camp. A series of flashbacks reveal Day's involvement in the devastating bombing of Germany and his experiences as a British prisoner of war in a German camp. Unable to cope with his complex feelings of grief, guilt and loss as well as with his memories of torture and near-starvation, Day has become mentally instable. He is aware of a "numb gap he could tell was asleep inside him. Something else had been there once, but he couldn't think what" (*Day* 35). By the time he returns to the UK, however, he has been able to overcome his guilt, and the novel ends on an optimistic note that implies potential future happiness for him and the woman he loves.

As both Barker's *Regeneration* trilogy and Kennedy's novel *Day* feature protagonists whose war experiences have left them deeply traumatized, various critics have discussed them as trauma fiction,[6] thus approaching the texts from a critical vantage point which is indebted to the work of trauma theorists such as Sigmund Freud, Cathy Caruth, Dominick LaCapra, and Shoshana Felman and Dori Laub. The novels' repeated use of flashbacks and their fluid change of narrative perspectives and focalization have been read as allowing the traumatic past to invade the present, thus doing justice to what

[4] All three novels are cited from the Viking omnibus edition of the trilogy.

[5] According to Elaine Showalter, 80,000 soldiers had been diagnosed with 'shell shock' by the end of World War One and 114,600 ex-servicemen applied for pensions on grounds of disorders related to 'shell shock' from 1919 to 1929 (168, 190). The term 'shell shock' was, however, a medical misnomer since the symptoms the term was used to describe neither resulted from being shelled nor were they always related to cases of shock (Showalter 168). For a detailed analysis of 'shell shock' as a cultural concept cf. Leese.

[6] Cf., for example, Bayer; Brannigan ("*Regeneration* Trilogy", *Pat Barker* 100-119); Mukherjee; Steveker; Vickroy (194-204); Whitehead (2004, *Trauma Fiction* 6 and passim).

Anne Whitehead has called the "haunting quality" of trauma (*Trauma Fiction* 12).[7] In contrast to such readings, which typically revolve around questions of how to "narrate the unnarratable" (*Trauma Fiction* 4) of "an event or experience which overwhelms the individual and resists language and representation" (*Trauma Fiction* 3), I will discuss Barker's *Regeneration* trilogy and Kennedy's *Day* with a view to the notion of precariousness which Judith Butler has put forth in her study *Precarious Life: The Powers of Mourning and Violence* (2004). Butler draws on Emmanuel Levinas in conceptualising the self as being both insolubly linked to and irrevocably different from the other: "One speaks, and one speaks for another, to another, and yet there is no way to collapse the distinction between the Other and oneself" (25). Due to the link that binds the self to the other, the former is called into responsibility for the latter. According to Butler, this responsibility "means to be awake to what is precarious in another life or, rather, the precariousness of life itself" (134). The ties to one's others, Butler argues,

> constitute what we are, ties or bonds that compose us. It is not as if an 'I' exists independently over here and then simply loses a 'you' over there, especially if the attachment to 'you' is part of what composes who 'I' am. If I lose you [...] then I not only mourn the loss, but become inscrutable to myself. (22)

Read within this ethical context, both Barker's and Kennedy's war novels turn out to be concerned, as I will argue, with narrating the violent loss of the other as an existential threat to the self. They centre on lives made precarious by the violence of war and the grief that follows from it. Following this approach, I will be able to avoid the trajectory inherent in trauma readings which progress towards the moment of healing when traumatized subjects, having succeeded in 'working through' their traumata, are able to reintegrate their experiences into their life stories. By contrast, my ethical reading will show how the literary texts under discussion represent war as disrupting the self's relation to the other, thus endangering one's hold onto one's own self.[8]

II

During their active service, the protagonist of the *Regeneration* trilogy and the main character of *Day* are repeatedly faced with losing fellow soldiers to whom the war has made them feel connected. Prior's position as an officer has caused him to become personally attached to the men under his command. With Prior's psychiatrist Rivers

[7] Cf. Bayer's analysis of the changing narrative perspectives in *Day* which "allow insight into Day's inner life and reveal that his war memories continue to dominate his life. [...] The very idea of the pastness of the past evaporates in the omnipresence of memories that interconnect historical moments and thereby make present those aspects of the past that Day has not yet successfully worked through" (168-169). Also cf. Brannigan who argues that "[i]n the *Regeneration* trilogy, [...] history is represented as trauma, the effects of which tend to manifest themselves in figures and tropes of haunting" (*Pat Barker* 117).

[8] Trauma criticism often pursues its own ethical agenda as it investigates the literary conventions which make it possible to narrativize a traumatic event whilst respecting the uniqueness it has for the traumatized subject.

serving as the narrative's focalizer, *Regeneration* describes the relationship between officers such as Prior and soldiers as being charged with parental affection and concern:

> Rivers had often been touched by the way in which young men, some of them not yet twenty, spoke about feeling like fathers to their men. [...] One of the paradoxes of the war – one of the many – was that this most brutal of conflicts should set up a relationship between officers and men that was . . . domestic. Caring. (97)

It is the brutal and senseless death of two men Prior cares for in this way which triggers his breakdown. The two soldiers called Sawdon and Towers are killed by a single shell while they are making tea in a fire bay during the early hours of a "quiet day" otherwise devoid of fighting (93). They die mere moments after Prior, walking by on trench watch, had "stopped to chat for a few minutes, and Towers [... had] offered him tea" (93). Although Prior's relationship with Sawdon and Towers is not spelled out in detail, the text evokes the impression of a personal bond between them. Mentioning the soldiers' names, the novel not only individualizes human suffering, but also personalizes the officer's connection to the two men. The chat and the offer of tea imply easy familiarity between them. Sawdon and Towers are also described as "*his* men" (94; emphasis added), with the possessive pronoun indicating the responsibility Prior feels for them.[9] As people to whom Prior is personally attached, Sawdon and Towers thus represent (two of) the others who constitute Prior's self.

The text relates in unsettling detail the complete bodily destruction of these two people. After the shell has hit them, there is "not much [left] of Sawdon and Towers" except for "flesh and splinters of blackened bone" and a single eyeball which Prior shovels into a sandbag in an effort to clean the trench (93). Having thus been drastically confronted with the extreme vulnerability to which war exposes human life, Prior loses his voice and his memory:

> he wanted to say something casual, something that would prove he was all right, but a numbness had spread all over the lower half of his face. [...] Back in the [...] clearing station he [...] tried to think back over the events that had brought him here, but found he could remember very little about them. Two of his men were dead, he remembered that. Nothing else. (94)

The violent death of the two soldiers, caused by the same war that has made Prior establish a personal connection to them, makes him undergo a severe crisis. Unable to access his own recent past, Prior has become "inscrutable" to himself, to use Butler's term (22).

It is, however, not only the death of Sawdon and Towers which begins to unravel the ties that hold together the relationality of Prior's self. While the process of unravelling seems to have been momentarily stalled in *Regeneration* when Prior regains his speech and, more importantly, his memory with the help of Rivers, it starts again, and more forcefully so, in *The Eye in the Door*. Reading the casualty lists over lunch in a London

9 When Prior himself talks about Sawdon and Towers as "my men" (95), the responsibility he feels for them is again emphasized.

pub crowded by civilians, Prior learns of the death of Captain James "Jimmy" Hore, a fellow officer he instantly felt connected to upon their first meeting (313-314). Feeling "very angry because Jimmy was dead, and ... everybody [in the pub] was enjoying themselves" (401), Prior indulges in bloody fantasies: he "would have liked nothing better, at that moment, than for a tank to come crashing through the doors [of the pub] and crush everybody [...]. The violence of his imaginings – he saw severed limbs, heard screams – terrified him" (314). After his gory vision, he suddenly finds himself back at his desk in his office, realising that he does not know how he came to be there: "Three hours had passed since he broke for lunch, and of that he could account for perhaps twenty to twenty-five minutes. The rest was blank" (314). This event adds to our understanding of how Barker's war novels negotiate an ethical concept of selfhood in which the vulnerability of the other calls into question the stability of the self. The anger Prior feels upon learning of Hore's death renders him "ec-static", a condition which Butler defines as follows: "To be ec-static means, literally, to be outside oneself, and this can have several meanings: to be transported beyond oneself by a passion, but also to be *beside oneself* with rage or grief" (24, emphasis in the original). During his visit to the pub, Prior can be seen as being beside himself with both grief at Hore's death and raging anger in the face of civilians whose oblivious ignorance of the violent reality of war he has come to hate and despise. According to Butler, "grief displays [...] the thrall in which our relations with others hold us, [...] in ways that often interrupt the self-conscious account of ourselves we might try to provide" (23). Caught up in his grief for Jimmy Hore, Prior fails to account for anything he might have done for almost three hours. He has once more become inscrutable to himself. Thus, the loss of Hore, who represents one of Prior's others, signifies yet another loosening of the ties which constitute Prior's self. It is therefore the vulnerability of others, the precariousness of their lives, which makes the self lose its autonomy and self-control in Barker's World War One trilogy.

The gap in Prior's memory is later revealed to have been one of several experiences of dissociation during which a second personality usurps Prior's consciousness (401). As the scene in the pub shows, this personality seizes control when Prior is rendered 'ec-static' by his grief for other people. Its actual creation, however, goes back to Prior being confronted with the vulnerability of his own life. As the 'other' Prior explains: "'I was born two years ago. In a shell-hole in France. [...] He [Prior] was wounded. He knew he had to go on. And he couldn't. So I came'" (395-396). It is through this figure of the double, with whom Prior shares his body, but not his consciousness, that the novel adds an internal dimension to its conception of the relational self. As I have argued elsewhere, Barker's trilogy draws on Stevenson's gothic novella *Strange Case of Dr Jekyll and Mr Hyde* (1886), thus depicting Prior's second personality as an "internal other" (Steveker 28).[10] Both Prior and his therapist Rivers repeatedly refer to Stevenson's protagonist when they talk about Prior's "*other* state" (321, emphasis in the original). Having told Rivers about his dissociation, Prior asks him: "You've read Jekyll and Hyde?" (322). Rivers in turn notices how his patient "spoke of looking at his hands to make sure they had not been transformed into the hairy hands of Hyde" (328); and he

[10] The following short analysis of the intertextual references to Stevenson's novella is based on Steveker (28-32).

contemplates that "[i]t was odd how the term 'Jekyll and Hyde' had passed into the language, so that even people who had never read Stevenson's story used the names as a shorthand for internal divisions" (328).

In both Stevenson's novella and Barker's trilogy, the figure of the internal other negotiates the loss of autonomy and self-control the respective protagonist experiences. But while Stevenson has Jekyll kill himself, thus containing the cultural anxiety which the notion of multiple selfhood evoked in the late nineteenth century, Barker affirms the notion of the multiple, and indeed relational, self. According to Rivers, the existence of the self is not called into question because self and internal other co-exist within one and the same individual. He contends that "contrary to what was usually supposed, *duality* was a *stable* state; the attempt at integration, dangerous" (392, emphasis added). Rivers argues that internal difference only destabilizes selfhood if there is no link between self and internal other. His colleague Henry Head is, for example, able to cope with difference because his self and his internal other have access to each other: "Head's dissociation was healthy because the researcher and the physician each had instant access to the experience of the other, and both had access to Head's experience in all other areas of his life" (330). By contrast, "Prior's [dissociation] was pathological because areas of his conscious experience had become inaccessible to memory" (330).

Looking at Rivers's psychological argument through the lens of ethics, I would argue that *The Eye in the Door* embraces the notion of the self's relationality. It is not the existence of internal otherness that endangers the self in the novel. But if the self is cut loose from its internal other(s), it becomes precariously instable and, to adopt Butler's phrase, inscrutable to itself. Whenever Prior's internal other takes over his consciousness, Prior literally does not know himself anymore. Not only is he forced to yield control over his body, but he is also unable to access the other Prior's memory. As his internal other puts it, "he [Prior] doesn't know anything I know" (394).

III

The notions of the self's unknowingness, its disruption and precariousness also feature strongly in A. L. Kennedy's novel *Day*. Although Kennedy's text focuses on World War Two and, therefore, on an altogether different moment in time, *Day* resembles Barker's trilogy in that it, too, confronts the reader with a detailed account of human suffering brought about by the violence of war. And like Billy Prior in the *Regeneration* trilogy, the titular hero of Kennedy's novel also experiences the war as endangering his sense of self as it implicates him in the precariousness of the lives of others. Alfred Day is presented as a deeply insecure young man to whom the war has offered the opportunity not only to leave his old life behind, but also to set up meaningful relationships to other people. Having volunteered for service "before he was called up" (43), he trains as an RAF tail-gunner and forms close bonds to the other members of his air crew:

> They were the crew and nothing other than the crew and that would be for ever and they'd have their picture taken to prove it, the family of them together.
> [...] they were building something like a family – the kind they'd ask for if they'd ever

> had the choice [...] and he knew he believed it, trusted, understood it wasn't only a war thing, that it was permanent. They were his crew. (66, 107)

Except for Day, his crew members die on one of their bombing trips to Hamburg when their Lancaster plane is hit by German flak. Their death is rendered as follows:

> *Flak* [...] *comes again and yo hear the skipper yo can tell it's him and there's other things yo hear like hurt babbies* [...] *and someone blarting for their ma* [...] *and that other thing on the floor that bad thing that might be the Bastard part of the Bastard* [...] *and now there is Miles there's this creature they made of Miles* [...] *and it's like a poor* [...] *lickle dog that's crouched with no chest* [...] *and you've got to see your skipper soon you need him or Dickie Molloy* [...] *to not be alone* [...] *and here he is yer skipper yer safety yer best yer gaffer and* [...] *his mask off and lollin and wet and he's took poorly took terrible badly [...] and his flying helmet tore open and red in his hair* [...] *and Parks is gone and Molloy and they've left their red behind and yo behind* [...]. (242-243, italics in the original)

This scene is by no means the only one in the novel which spells out the brutalities of World War Two. There are others which relate a death march of prisoners in Germany,[11] the mass slaughter committed by a Waffen SS division in Latvia[12] and the brutal murder of German civilians by Soviet troops.[13] Nevertheless, the loss of Day's crew is central to my reading of Kennedy's text since it is the death of these soldiers that the whole story of Day's unravelling self centres on. The long, convoluted stream-of-consciousness sentence quoted above serves to mediate the violence of the men's annihilation as directly as possible. It also shows that Day feels left behind when they die. For him, their death is, above all, his loss.

According to Butler the self loses itself when it loses its other(s): "I have lost 'you' only to discover that 'I' have gone missing myself" (22); the grieving self "is called into question by its relation to its Other, a relation that does not precisely reduce me to

[11] In one of his flashbacks, Day recalls a German soldier murdering a woman on a death march: "The woman in the forest when they were marching, when the Germans were pushing them west; she had a man with her and wanted his help, there on her knees and blood on her and shouting because he should help her [...] and the man doing nothing, of course, being dead already and her screaming in German at a German soldier and him raising his gun to make her stop" (46).

[12] At the film set, Day meets a man called Vasyl who tells him that he, having become a member of a Latvian Waffen SS division, wilfully took part in massacres: "I hit a female first. Only because of the noise she was making. [...] I hit her six, seven times, because in the beginning you can't stop. [...] We did that first killing almost until sunset. Mainly in the square. I fell once, because of the blood. [...] the best is to take them out alive and make them dig graves [...] – I killed all types" (222-223).

[13] Day remembers "walking into the house with the blue window frames, neatly done, the place where the Russians had called and got drunk: Alfred [Day] hadn't known what to expect before he saw: broken things in the good front room, the foreign kind of parlour, and where they'd lit a fire on the rug and the hair, meat and hair, hidden under the kitchen table [...] Her breasts, she'd been cut on her breasts. The child cut, too. Beyond recognising" (46).

speechlessness, but does nevertheless clutter my speech with signs of its undoing" (23). Butler's argument provides a particularly apt perspective for an ethical reading of Kennedy's novel, since the war and, in particular, the loss of his others have caused Day to "lo[se] himself" (*Day* 35). What is more, the whole narrative structure of the text invites us to see Day as a self who is made precarious as the ties to his others are cut loose. The novel alternates between narrative times as well as between three different narrative perspectives. It jumps abruptly between past, present and future, and it equally abruptly changes between a first-person, a second-person and a third-person narrator. In this confusing montage of scenes and voices, Day alternatively functions as an autodiegetic narrator, as the internal focalizer of heterodiegetic narration and as a voice addressing itself in 'you-narrative'. Sometimes teetering on the brink of becoming incomprehensible, the text thus represents a self who is in danger of being undone by the undoing of its relations to its others. In her review of *Day*, Ursula Le Guin has taken issue with the novel's narrative structure: "'I' reverts to 'he', in the conventional third person narration that began the novel. Then suddenly 'he' becomes 'you' again. This constant shifting between three narrative modes, one of them highly artificial, ensures that the author's stylistic self-consciousness dominates the book". What Le Guin misses here is that the three different narrative perspectives serve to depict a self whom the war has caused to disintegrate. This process of unravelling is most pronounced in the scenes which depict the first time of Day's imprisonment in Germany, beginning directly after his crew's death:

> Dulag Luft: that should be where you're taken, but you don't think you're there. [...] They don't say where you are and you can't see. There's only this room and the other. [...]
> *I was always wrong.* [...] – *I was made inside me to be wrong. And* [...] *yo fucking knock that out of a boy, yo bate him tell he doe feel it and yo knock him right.* [...]
> There is only this room and the other. [...] The other room is where it's your fault you get a beating. [...] Sometimes rubber truncheons, sometimes leather with a sting in them [...]. Sometimes you don't see. Not interested. [...] While you stand, there's this crying you do sometimes. [...] They see names in your face and then try to smack them out.
> *Yo cor ave em, though – or me.* [...]
> There is only this room and the other. [...]
> They threw him back eventually – he was too small a fish. And the Luftwaffe guards came and took him [...]. They gave him a number and a tag [...], a blanket and a Red Cross parcel, all of his very own to keep. [...] he wasn't ashamed by anything [...]. (248-252, italics in the original)

Each narrative mode provides Day's own perspective, but by positing him not only as 'I', but also as 'you' and 'he', the text shows Day as having lost contact to himself. Existing side by side, the novel's three narrative perspectives serve to frame the precariousness of a self whose relationality has been disrupted by war in both its external and internal dimensions. What is more, the novel's 'you-narrative' also addresses its readers, thus connecting them to the protagonist. Putting readers into Day's place, the novel prevents them from approaching Day's story from the comfortable position of the voyeuristic consumer.[14] Instead, it implicates the reader in the protagonist's vulnerability. Rendering Day as the 'you', that is the other, the text ascribes to the reader the position of the 'I', that is the self, who cannot withdraw from the other's suffering.

IV

As I have argued above, both the *Regeneration* trilogy and *Day* negotiate war as making life precarious in that the violence it inflicts upon humans is shown as hacking away at the self's ties to its external and internal others. Barker's and Kennedy's narrations of war foreground individuals whose selves are made precarious by the vulnerability of others' lives. Thus, the texts' protagonists do not appear as subjects whose traumata violate their autonomy. Instead they represent relational selves who are affected by the suffering of others. The wars they take part in subject Billy Prior and Alfred Day to processes in which the loss of the other and the grief that follows from it leave the self 'dis-composed', as it were. Nevertheless, both Barker's and Kennedy's protagonists reach a point at which they are able to stop their disintegration. In *The Eye in the Door*, Rivers encourages Billy to accept his internal other: "There has to be a moment of . . . recognition. Acceptance. There has to be a moment when you look into the mirror and say, yes, this too is myself" (402). Rivers's words echo those of Jekyll who sees Hyde in a mirror and states: "This, too, was myself" (Stevenson 58). But unlike Stevenson's protagonist, Prior succeeds in accepting his internal other. While Jekyll commits suicide once the initial euphoria that accompanied Hyde's creation has turned into complete and utter rejection, Prior is able to acknowledge the difference within himself. However, although the reader learns, at the end of *The Eye in the Door*, that Prior has been successful in his efforts of acceptance (420), the actual moment of recognition is not narrated. Its absence from the text indicates that this moment does not entail a narrative process in which a traumatized subject reintegrates the traumatic experience into his life-story. Instead, Prior's acceptance of his internal other is an ethical act in the Levinasian sense. Levinas points out that the self's relation with the other "certainly consists in wanting to understand him" (5), but he problematizes understanding as "an act of violence and of negation. A partial negation, which is violence" (9). Although Levinas talks about the external other, his notion of understanding as violence is helpful in order grasp the ethical implications of Prior recognizing his "malignant double" (*Eye* 328). Rivers's recommendation to "look into the mirror and say, yes, this too is myself" (402) indicates that Prior does not need to understand his internal other in order to accept him. The look into the mirror suggests acknowledgement rather than understanding. As Prior does not negate otherness, but succeeds in accepting it, his 'moment of recognition' respects the other in his difference and is, therefore, devoid of violence. This notion of recognition does not imply the reintegration of the other into the self. It enables the self to re-affirm its relationality as it reforms its connection to the other. Barker's trilogy thus sustains the notion of the multiple, relational self, even though its protagonist is able to "heal the split" (402), thus stopping the unravelling of his self.

[14] Gabriele Rippl discusses a similar strategy in A. L. Kennedy's first novel *Looking for the Possible Dance* (225).

In Kennedy's novel, the protagonist also succeeds in healing the split in his personality, but he does so in a fundamentally different way. On his last evening as a film extra, Day sings "Jerusalem" in front of other members of the film crew:

> Alfred standing and the sound like alive in him now and round him, tilting his head and wrapping him with a light he only touches, cannot see.
> And he can believe that he hears Pluckrose singing, that lovely awful voice, and they are here together again [...].
> And he can believe that he hears the Bastard and Molloy and Torrington and Miles and Parks and they are back and didn't die.
> And he can believe the he hears his skipper. His skipper.
> And he can believe that if he opens up his eyes the benches will be full of the boys lost to the sky and his friends the closest, his crew the closest, so near he can take their hands and know they are well and never were harmed and never were frightened, never lost.
> And he can believe that he is forgiven.
> He can believe so much, the truth of it makes him weep. (263)

Enabling him to shed his guilt, this cathartic moment allows Day to envision himself as being once more in the company of those he lost in the war. Like Prior, he, too, seems to have re-established the relations to his others. However, the change in the novel's narrative structure which follows upon this scene makes clear that Day's experience represents an act of reintegration. While the novel's third but last chapter, which ends with Day's performance, still contains all three narrative perspectives, its penultimate chapter does not include any autodiegetic narration. Except for a very few lines, the last chapter exclusively features the 'you-narrative'. If the three different perspectives represent, as I have argued, Day's disrupted personality, the absence of first one and then two of these perspectives represents his (re)united identity. Having its protagonist reintegrate his self and others into a single whole, Kennedy's novel clearly – and without any irony – draws on liberal-humanist ideologies. With Alfred unifying his self by singing a piece of the high-cultural British musical canon, this scene furthermore smacks of the same cultural elitism that critics have identified in Ian McEwan's novel *Saturday* in which a young woman saves herself by reciting Matthew Arnold's "Dover Beach" to her would-be-rapist (Eckstein 7-10). Although *Day* and the *Regeneration* trilogy share similar interests in narrating the precariousness of life, Kennedy's text in the end rejects the notion of the self's relationality which it explores. In contrast to Barker's *Regeneration* trilogy, which privileges a concept of multiple, relational selfhood, Kennedy's novel represents the process of healing her protagonist undergoes as integration of self and other-than-self into liberal-humanist unity. The fact that even authors as critically aware as A. L. Kennedy put forward constructions of unified, self-sufficient male selfhood gives evidence to the strong hold that this concept and its ideological tenets still have on the British cultural imaginary at the beginning of the twenty-first century.

Works Cited

Bayer, Gerd. "World War II Fiction and the Ethics of Trauma." *Ethics and Trauma in Contemporary British Fiction*. Ed. Susana Onega and Jean-Michel Ganteau. Amsterdam: Rodopi, 2011. 155-174.

Barker, Pat. *The Regeneration Trilogy: Regeneration, The Eye in the Door, The Ghost Road.* London: Viking, 1996.

Brannigan, John. *Pat Barker*. Manchester: Manchester University Press, 2005.

—. "Pat Barker's *Regeneration* Trilogy." *Contemporary British Fiction*. Ed. Richard J. Lane, Rod Mengham and Philip Tew. Cambridge: Polity Press, 2003. 13-26.

Butler, Judith. *Precarious Life: The Powers of Mourning and Violence*. London: Verso, 2004.

Eckstein, Lars. "Saturday on Dover Beach: Ian McEwan, Matthew Arnold, and post-9/11 Melancholia." *Hard Times* 89.1 (2011): 6-10.

Kennedy, A. L. *Day*. 2007. London: Vintage, 2008. Kindle edition.

Korte, Barbara and Ralf Schneider. "Introduction." *War and the Cultural Construction of Identities in Britain*. Ed. Korte and Schneider. Amsterdam: Rodopi, 2002. 1-8.

Leese, Peter. *Shell Shock: Traumatic Neurosis and the British Soldiers of the First World War.* Basingstoke: Palgrave Macmillan, 2002.

Le Guin, Ursula. "At War With You." *The Guardian* 7 April 2007. Retrieved 16 Sep. 2013. http://www.theguardian.com/books/2007/apr/07/fiction.alkennedy.

Levinas, Emmanuel. *Entre Nous: On Thinking-of-the-Other*. Trans. Michael B. Smith and Barbara Harshav. London: Athlone Press, 2000.

Mukherjee, Ankhi. "Stammering to Story: Neurosis and Narration in Pat Barker's Regeneration." *Critique: Studies in Contemporary Fiction* 43.1 (2001): 49-62.

Rippl, Gabriele. "'Naked in the Grip of Reality' – A. L. Kennedys Ästhetik der Gewalt." *Gewalt, Geschlecht, Fiktion: Gewaltdiskurse und Gender-Problematik in zeitgenössischen englischsprachigen Romanen, Dramen und Filmen*. Ed. Susanne Bach. Trier: WVT, 2009. 221-238.

Rommel, Thomas. "'Lines Suggested by the War in the Crimea': Florence Nightingale and the Individual Soldier." *War and the Cultural Construction of Identities in Britain*. Ed. Barbara Korte and Ralf Schneider. Amsterdam: Rodopi, 2002. 109-123.

Steveker, Lena. "Reading Trauma in Pat Barker's *Regeneration* Trilogy." *Ethics and Trauma in Contemporary British Fiction*. Ed. Susana Onega and Jean-Michel Ganteau. Amsterdam: Rodopi, 2011. 21-36.

Stevenson, Robert Louis. *Strange Case of Dr Jekyll and Mr Hyde*. 1886. London: Penguin, 2002.

Showalter, Elaine. *The Female Malady: Women, Madness and English Culture, 1830-1980*. 1985. London: Virago, 1987.

Vickroy, Laurie. *Trauma and Survival in Contemporary Fiction*. Charlottesville: University of Virginia Press, 2002. 192-204.

Whitehead, Anne. *Trauma Fiction*. Edinburgh: Edinburgh University Press, 2004.

—. "Open to Suggestion: Hypnosis and History in Pat Barker's *Regeneration*." *Critical Perspectives on Pat Barker*. Ed. Sharon Monteith et al. Columbia: University of South Carolina Press, 2005. 203-218.

Barbara Kowalczuk

The Texture of Devastation: Philip Jones Griffiths's Vietnam Trilogy

1. Gazes

Welsh photographer Philip Jones Griffiths (1936-2008) arrived in Vietnam in the summer of 1966 on his first commission for Magnum. On stepping off the plane, he instantly felt like an exile returning home at last. There were haunting similarities between the Vietnam hamlets he visited and the Welsh village where he had grown up, and Griffiths could not help being reminded of the repeated invasions of Wales by the English, and the subsequent cultural annihilation his own people had undergone. This first impression intensified as he travelled around South Vietnam and came to realize that what he was in fact witnessing was a genocidal war, combined with unprecedented environmental destruction. Such insights drove Griffiths to "concentrate on showing the human face of conflict" (Griffiths qtd. in Brockway), but it was not until 1980 that he eventually managed to meet the first Agent Orange victims. His photojournalism would expose the de-humanization of those people, who had heretofore been seen both by the military and American public opinion as inscrutable Orientals, foreign 'others', often reduced to the derogatory terms referring to them – *gooks*, *dicks*, *dinks*.

A self-proclaimed anti-war photographer, Griffiths made more than twenty return visits to Vietnam and worked on numerous projects that focused on post-war life there. His seminal work, *Vietnam Inc.* (1971), which had strongly contributed to alerting the Americans to the horrors of the conflict, was followed by the publication of *Agent Orange: "Collateral Damage" in Viet Nam* (2003) and *Viet Nam at Peace* (2005). The three books now compose what I call Griffiths's Vietnam Trilogy. Griffiths captured on film devastated landscapes and civilians, but also the fragile process of post-war reconstruction. His photographs show Napalm and Agent Orange victims – alive, dead or unborn – as well as the extreme poverty of the survivors, made even worse in their wrecked urban or natural environment. *Agent Orange* exposes the disastrous side effects of the war on a land that was bombed, napalmed and sprayed with toxic chemicals for the most part of the duration of the war (1964-1973). As for *Viet Nam at Peace*, although it opens with images of people swept by a "flush of jubilation" (24) as they celebrate the end of the conflict, it also reveals the permanent marks left both on the land and on the flesh of its inhabitants.

This chapter was mostly inspired by influential essays on photography. While using some of Roland Barthes's concepts, I draw mainly, however, on a remark made by Susan Sontag in *On Photography*. In the chapter entitled "In Plato's Cave", Sontag attributes the shock provoked by some photographs to their novelty in our representational culture, adding that such shock might become a rarity in the future due to the mass-production of appalling images. When novelty is still a possibility, Sontag claims that "[o]ne's first encounter with the photographic inventory of ultimate horror is a kind of revelation, the prototypically modern revelation: a negative epiphany" (*On Photography* 19). I want to focus on the procedures through which Griffiths's photographic objects often trigger one such "prototypically modern revelation", although in a quaint fashion. Indeed, I argue that the "inventory of ultimate horror" provokes in fact a *deferred* "negative epiphany". Another significant inspiration on my work was a comment made by Jean Kempf in respect of Garry Winogrand's photographs, which Kempf analyses as setting up an "exchange of gazes, an eye to eye, just like one would say a face to face" (173; my translation).[1] It is precisely such "eye-to-eye" exchanges that I intend to study in Griffiths's work: how the implicit network sketched by the characters' gazes may *retrospectively* affect the viewer's perception of the photographs. I propose therefore to capture what I call the texture of devastation, devastation as it is represented in the Vietnam Trilogy, and the procedures through which this weaving of gazes manages to affect ultimately the *viewer*'s gaze.

To Philip Jones Griffiths,

> Vietnam was the most intense experience imaginable, and one that was filled with a kind of macabre humor, which of course didn't detract from the tragedy of the whole thing. But most of the time, it was the ultimate clash of civilizations – the wise, smart little David running around, irritating the hell out of this huge Goliath. (Howe)

The "clash of civilizations" that was part of the harrowing experience is definitely what *Vietnam Inc.*, the first volume of the Trilogy, seeks to put in images. Griffiths's 'photo-essay' opens with a short text in which the author condemns the US doctrine and politics in Vietnam. Viewing the war as a dramatic encounter between the West and the East, Griffiths pins the blame of the massacre of an alien people and culture on the Americans' deficiencies and lack of wisdom, as well as on their determination to impose their values – or "brand" (12), as he puts it in *Viet Nam at Peace* – and to outcompete the communist enemy.

A mesmerizing, full-page portrait of an unhelmeted American soldier sitting with a little Vietnamese girl on his lap, strongly suggestive of friendship, follows this indictment, making it clear that to Griffiths the slaughter of the Vietnamese people was perpetrated for wrong reasons. The black-and-white photograph is printed with no caption, unlike most pictures in the rest of the volume. Both subjects have an eerie gaze which Harrison sees as being "accompanied by a scream of rage". At a structural level, the portrait underlines the machinery of photographic representation, of the placement of signs before the viewer's eyes, made possible by the mediation of the photographer's mechanical device. At the level of our reception of those signs, however, a reversed relationship is prompted. The viewer's gaze is returned by the staring eyes of the two characters, as if the viewer were in turn framed by the subjects' gazes.

Retrospectively, this discomforting stare even appears to be ominous, as it invites comparison with other images taken later by Griffiths, which likewise give the uncanny

[1] Originally, "un échange de regards, un œil à œil comme l'on dirait un face à face" (173).

impression that the subjects' piercing gazes tangibly target the camera eye, reflecting therefore the presence of both the photographer and the future viewers. Retrospectively, when the picture which opens *Vietnam Inc.* is seen again from the perspective of the whole Trilogy, it gains new momentum. The viewer's gaze is so to speak intensified, forced to accommodate a supplementary meaning, which expresses no longer friendship, but the horrendous consequences of the American intervention in Vietnam. For example, it suddenly dawns on the viewer that the little girl might be the sole survivor of a village devastated by the American troops, an orphan whose parents have just been killed by the soldiers. Rage, grief, or even guilt now start to alter the narrative that is always implicit in any photographic image. As he/she looks at the photograph, the viewer is thus forced to experience different levels of temporality, while being invited to grasp the uniqueness of the past moment, the 'that-has-been' captured on film.

In Barthes's theory, the 'that-has-been' ("ça-a-été"; cf. Barthes Chapter 32) is the very essence of photography. Barthes insists on the interaction between reality and the past: "something *landed* before the little hole and remained there forever" (123-124; my translation).[2] To him, the 'that-has-been' presents 'a reality' which transports the viewer into the past. This temporal movement evokes to Barthes the return of the dead, and accounts for the haunting spectrality of the past moment captured on film. Here, the soldier and the little girl give the impression that they are aware of being on the verge of being turned into 'objects' of the photograph for the future viewer to look at them, as at a past reality. What is more, although they look straight into the camera eye, they also express through their war-weary bodies some kind of withdrawal, which leaves us with the feeling that they are also, to some extent, experiencing their own death, their own fading from their own present moment. Finally, as the war is still raging outside, and we have now been made aware of the carnage that was going on outside the hut, on retrospect, we are also made to feel that this photograph conjugates death in the future perfect tense, integrating a form of déjà vu in reverse, the foreknowledge of a devastation which will have already happened when the viewer ultimately receives the image. Of course, the same phenomenon is at work when we look at the other pictures, insofar as they take us back to this initial portrait and make us feel the extent of the disastrous effects of the war.

Yet, the photograph remains a 'poor' image, inasmuch as it cannot encapsulate the sensory, cognitive and emotional motivations that induced the photographer to fix the moment on film. The original perceptions and intentions are absolutely lost and unretrievable for the viewer. The pose of the soldier and the girl is a frozen instant which lays emphasis on the fragile and ephemeral relationship between the two characters, as well as on the photographer's and the viewer's tentative effort of communication with them. In other words, the image initiates a war narrative – in fact a multiplicity of equally plausible war narratives – which are all bound to remain incomplete and to frustrate the viewer's desire to 'communicate' with the two characters. The relationship between Griffiths and his two characters started before and may have continued after the photograph was taken, but the image is silent about such moments. It is therefore only with hindsight, when it is implicitly linked with the other photographs which expose the horror of the war in the rest of the Trilogy, that this image triggers a "negative

[2] "[Q]uelque chose *s'est posé* devant le petit trou et y est resté à jamais" (123-124).

epiphany" and retrospectively shocks the viewer. This deferred revelation is made possible only if all the pictures of survivors and victims have been seen at some point. Griffiths's gazes are thus what might be called 'intericonic' gazes: they are the metonymic details that bind the images together, granting them a surplus of signification.

In my view, that is why most portraits presented in the Trilogy evince some kind of withdrawal from and inattention to the present, as if the subjects were suspended in time and lost in their own psychic spaces. As a matter of fact, the initial look-forwardness of *Vietnam Inc.*'s gazes is gradually replaced in the Trilogy by blank gazes or no gazes at all, especially in the photographs of Napalm and Agent Orange victims. Griffiths's post-war pictures of physically and mentally handicapped children living in "a private world of smiles and screams" (Griffiths, *Agent Orange* 108) do indeed constitute a collection of dazed and enigmatic expressions, and the horrendous photographs of eyeless children sitting on their mother's laps or lying on their beds in orphanages do again precipitate a "negative epiphany", which still complicates our reception of the photograph inaugurating *Vietnam Inc.*, as the photographic traces of the desolation caused by Agent Orange are *virtually* included in this first picture, metamorphosing the little Vietnamese girl's and the soldier's gazes into a premonitory image of the future war's side-effects.

Griffiths and his subjects stand therefore as precarious witnesses of the horrors of the Vietnam War. The survivors of Agent Orange spraying literally *embody* the dehumanizing process of modern, chemical warfare, but most of them can no longer *see* the desolation resulting from the war. They are therefore paradoxical witnesses, survivors who at the same time are not quite witnesses, since they have not seen the whole action of the war and cannot therefore turn it into a narrative, which would imply a beginning, a middle and an end. According to Agamben, "*superstes* designates a person who has lived through something, who has experienced an event from beginning to end and can therefore bear witness to it" (17). The Agent Orange victims stand as blind *superstes*, who cannot speak either, narrate the disaster they have been subjected to. In fact, they have become *superstes* simply because Griffiths decided to keep a trace of their past catastrophe, and to record the enduring effects of the devastation, still impacting the present. The image becomes an archive, but one which metamorphoses the photographer himself into a *superstes*, in his own way.

Of course, Griffiths never experienced any war trauma, nor was he poisoned by chemicals, but he spent years working in Vietnam, witnessing the atrocities committed during the war, as well as the war aftermath. On numerous occasions, he was even the first photographer to enter the villages of the damned and take pictures of the survivors. His long-lasting involvement and concern for the future of Vietnam led him to establish close relationships with the medical authorities. His series of the fetuses kept in specimen jars at the Tu Du hospital in Ho Chi Minh City was considered as a groundbreaking work that allowed him to show one of the most horrifying impacts of the war. To a certain extent, it might be said, therefore, that Griffiths's photographs supplied the blind victims with the eyes that were necessary for the survivors to be also witnesses. In any case, they are evidence that he was still there after the tragedy, very often the only surviving witness.

His portraits of Agent Orange and Napalm victims acquire thus what might be called a 'monumental' presence, turned, as an interconnected whole, into a memorial, which as such inevitably provokes the viewer's emotional involvement. When looking back, the portrait of the soldier sitting with the little girl on his lap is indeed endowed with a spectral dimension, the vacant eyes of the two characters seeming to be proleptic of the empty gazes of the living-dead haunting the villages through which Griffiths would wander years after the war had ended. Their eyes no longer tell us a story of friendship and reconciliation; they become poignant, pierce our hearts, puncture our gazes, blind us too, bruise us, each wound, each maimed or half-formed limb also acting on the viewer's gaze in the fashion of Barthes's *punctum*: "[t]he *punctum* of the photograph [...] pricks me (but also bruises me, is poignant to me)" (49; my translation)[3] The photographic collection of the human monsters preserved in formaldehyde shocks us because it "bruises" our gaze, affects us and makes us too into precarious beings, potentially vulnerable witnesses.

But it is the accumulation of war and post-war images which makes the viewer experience in a vicarious way the historical and personal trauma which such pictures represent. The pictures acquire intensity and precipitate a traumatic effect which may in fact be apprehended only afterwards, once such pictures have been mentally connected to one another, in their 'intericonicity'. As he/she browses through the volumes of the Trilogy, the viewer is turned into what I call a sign digger who may finally achieve a more complete vision of war and unveil the deeper meanings of the photographs. This is what Lauzon proposes to call the "trans-opacity of the photographic sign" (188). And Sontag is quite right when she says that one should never be content with "the surface" of photography: "Any photograph has multiple meanings [...] The ultimate wisdom of the photographic image is to say: 'There is the surface. Now think – or rather feel, intuit – what is beyond it, what the reality must be like if it looks this way'" (*On Photography* 23). The Trilogy does indeed lend itself to being 'read' as an invitation to go beyond the surface, to cross the frames of the photographs, therefore, and explore their deeper meaning. For the act of receiving a photograph is not as passive one: by looking *actively* at the photographic sign, one may seize a more complete narrative.

Inevitably, such 'trans-opacity' is also what might give way to a partial understanding of Griffiths's work. Ideally, the Trilogy should precipitate a conflation of the photographer's gaze and fore-seeing, and of the viewer's subsequent act of looking. Yet, the photographs do not necessarily prompt a complete cognitive process leading to the full apprehension of their significance. Taken individually, each photograph may be characterized by its lack of stability, if only because sometimes the photographer's intentions remain unknown. The incongruity of the pastoral scene represented in "Limits of Friendship" (*Vietnam Inc.* 34-35) exemplifies this ambiguity. The image shows a Marine offering a cigarette to a young Vietnamese girl. The American is actually turning his back on the photographer and his facial expression is not visible. Griffiths's introduction to *Viet Nam at Peace* uncovers what for him triggered some sort of private mental 'intericonicity' when he shot the picture:

> In Viet Nam I saw parallels that to me, at least, seemed obvious. Even the sight of GI's handing out candy to Vietnamese children (part of the PsyOps programme) harked backed [*sic*] to my childhood. During WWII American soldiers were stationed at a nearby camp.

[3] "Le *punctum* d'une photo [...] me point (mais aussi me meurtrit, me poigne)" (49).

> One day they arrived at my school and for no reason started handing out Mars bars to everyone in the playground. I remember even then being suspicious of their motive. It made no sense. (11)

In "Limits of Friendship", the message is seemingly, at surface level, transparent. In the background – a very picturesque rural landscape – one perceives Vietnamese peasants working peacefully in a field, standing as blurred silhouettes. The picture focuses on the slightly decentered girl smiling at the American in combat gear, whose imposing stature contrasts with that of the frail child, in what seems to be a benevolent, protective attitude. However, Griffiths's recollection of his school days in Wales during WWII suggests that the photograph contains a degree of 'opacity', a hidden story that does not clearly unfold on film. Thus, depending on the viewer's knowledge of the context, which includes the photographer's private memories, the photograph's significance can be grasped, or missed. The original motivation of the photographer for shooting the picture forms a hidden subtext which remains opaque while the transparent storyline (a young Vietnamese befriending an American soldier) is immediately captured.

The photograph's caption, "Limits of Friendship", does not fully transcribe the irony meant by Griffiths. What is implied is that the American soldier's civic action is a rather vain attempt while all around them the carnage is going on. But since the caption is also a private reference to childhood memories, the key to a full interpretation of the picture is not to be found within the image itself, which includes its caption. What "makes sense" here is actually a non-sense ("it made no sense") felt years before the picture was taken. At first glance, the girl's smile evokes a situation that, to Griffiths at least, is the deceiving surface of the story. The *punctum* of the snapshot is then the Marine's rifle, pointing toward the sky. The weapon pricks the viewer's eye and prevents his/her perception of the seemingly trivial pastoral scene from being ahistorical. We see the rifle as an element that propels the act of seeing beyond the transparent sign (the smile) and therefore, out of the two framed subjects whose interaction in the photograph seems to tell the story of a budding friendship. When we focus on the weapon, however, we come to contemplate the possibility of a different narrative, one which unmistakably refers to the violence of war and the precariousness of all 'peaceful' moments. Signs of friendship are made to appear as symptoms of a distorted relationship, and of a fragile, vulnerable humanity. What was previously seen as a friendly act is turned into something "suspicious", to borrow Griffiths's word. Friendship has limits, indeed, and the American's motive becomes more uncertain, leading the viewer who is aware of Griffiths's explanation to think that there might also be some kind of manipulation and deception behind the supposedly friendly gesture – after all, is not introducing a young peasant girl to filter-tips an indication of something wrong going on?

"Limits of Friendship" is thus also a subtle statement about the impact the presence of the Americans had on the local inhabitants' culture, as they sought to impose their way of life on the Vietnamese. And indeed, in *Viet Nam at Peace*, Griffiths collected pictures which show to what extent the Vietnamese embraced consumerism. The cigarette that the soldier offers to the little girl stands therefore as one of the signs promising an "American-sponsored urban revolution" (12). Certainly, it is nothing more than a sign. When the viewer observes the photograph, time has passed and there is no knowing what happened afterwards to the subjects involved in the picture. Telling the full story is not the purpose of the photographer: the narrative initiated by this image denotes a moment of precariousness which contains the implied complexities of a dangerous and uncertain situation. Griffiths's photograph stands both as a *pulling* image – one that draws the viewer towards itself – and a *resisting* signifier – one which leaves the spectator on insecure hermeneutic grounds.

Commenting on the snapshot "Captured Suspects" (*Vietnam Inc.* 52-53), which shows chained Vietnamese prisoners, Griffiths emphasized in an interview the uncertain meaning of the image:

> I turned around and there was, well, there were these guys being laid off [...]. At that moment, he [an American soldier marching along the prisoners] put his hand up to his throat. I'm still not quite sure why [...]. They knew that they were in trouble [...]. I don't know why he put his hand ... it was just a reflexive gesture and I don't know whether he was ... I don't know. (Dannin, "Choking Photograph")

Griffiths's images are supposed to reveal his intention to show precarious lives, threatened by death, or handicap, during and after the war, but the way we receive such images of precariousness, as we have seen, greatly depends on the ability and the inclination of the viewers "to feast their eyes on the misery of others" (Taylor 13) and to capitalize on their grief or trauma. Photo-understanding is therefore never quite fully secured, whatever the captions or the ironic comments Griffiths may add to his pictures. Receptionability – the ability of the beholder to receive, accept and welcome the image – is definitely an essential phase in the life of any photograph, and it is important to assess the way the Vietnam Trilogy arouses "empathy with the violated" (Taylor 7).

2. Dis/Regarding the Pain of the Other

Griffiths's photo-essays raise of course numerous issues, including voyeurism and 'unphotographability'. Can the photographer show everything? Are all subjects photographable? What is the limit of decency for a war photographer? While the camera shoots straight into the heart of devastating precariousness, lives poisoned and destroyed by defoliant, it also runs the risk of shocking, perhaps even traumatizing in turn the viewer. Griffiths once claimed in an interview that "[j]ournalists should be by their very nature anarchists, people who want to point out things that are not generally approved of" (Dannin, "Anarchist Journalist"). Yet, when he published *Agent Orange* in 2003, he himself saw the limits of his own "anarchism", aware that his ghastly photographs of malformed fetuses stacked up in jars might cause readers to turn away and develop some kind of 'iconophobia':

> The problem with this book is that the pictures are so shocking, you can't look at it. I tried to put pictures in that have some humanity. The horrendous pictures of kids with genitalia on their faces, I didn't use. The truly horrendous pictures are not in there. ("Philip Jones Griffiths Discussing *Agent Orange*")

The dilemma was in fact ethical. The camera's intrusive, prying mechanical eye had to cross the threshold of inhumanity, not for the sake of provocation, but for the sake of information, which Griffiths felt to be his duty as a witness. To show the appalling aftermath of the Vietnam War, as it had been waged by the U.S., he had to go beyond the limits of the imaginable, and therefore take the risk to be himself emotionally devastated. The notion of unphotographability is of course related to the question of voyeurism and of "its implied sadism" (Taylor 13). But there are no such things as voyeurism and sadism in Griffiths's work. What is foregrounded, rather, is an interrogation concerning the use of the defoliant by the American army and the dramatic consequences on the land and the Vietnamese people.

The photographs included in *Agent Orange* were carefully selected by Griffiths, a process considerably affected by his interrogations regarding both the ethics of the gaze and the 'iconophobia' that might force him to abandon the publication of his photo-essay. Griffiths had to consider self-censorship; but then came the realization that repulsion had to be resisted, that showing the unphotographable was also a way of honouring both the dead and the living, a tribute to the tragedy of the stillborn and to the fortitude of the survivors as well. When "[g]iving birth becomes a game of roulette" (Griffiths, "Introduction"), the photographer cannot ignore such ethical obligation. In *Images in Spite of All*, Didi-Huberman considers the representability of the Holocaust as he analyzes four photographs taken by a Jewish prisoner in Auschwitz, in August 1944. Didi-Huberman insists that we "*are obliged* to that oppressive imaginable" (3). Griffiths's photographs of Agent Orange victims are such "images in spite of all": they remind those who did not suffer that they cannot shelter themselves by looking away.

Agent Orange forces us to acknowledge therefore that 'iconophobia' must be challenged, that unbearable images should not be deprived of visibility. The iconophobic gaze deceptively leads to the comfortable belief that a war crime can be disregarded. But there must be an empathic response to such inhumanity, as a recognition of the victims' existence. The unimaginable images demand to be deciphered in a private mental darkroom which allows one to reflect for a moment whether, and to what extent, he/she can bear to "regard", as Sontag puts it, "the pain of others".[4] The dreadfulness of the images comes from the fact that they show human beings turned into freaks, but by doing so they also highlight how both precious and precarious human life is.

Agent Orange is not a coffee table book, it does not entertain the viewer and it cannot be approached in a superficial way. Some people find it impossible to look at more than a couple of pictures because as they catch a glimpse of them, they discover a 'novelty', something they had never seen or imagined to exist before. Griffiths's photographs shock us because they force us to question our own status as human beings, to consider the animality within ourselves. Sontag interestingly compares the use of the camera to an implicitly aggressive act. Yet, she adds, it is this very aggression which actually serves to "democratize all experiences by translating them into images" (*On Photography* 7). Griffiths's photographs are pieces of evidence which "democratize" traumatic events by bearing witness to their consequences.

Agent Orange constitutes thus a pivotal volume in the Vietnam Trilogy, since the viewer is invited to see more to the images collected in the two remaining volumes,

[4] We refer here to Sontag's work *Regarding the Pain of Others.*

Vietnam Inc. and *Viet Nam at Peace*. In the final volume, the photographs of huge billboards, which betray the country's embrace of consumerism, are more than a social and economic statement on the nation's post-war evolution. There is a feeling of uneasiness that emerges from looking at such images because they contrast, sometimes in an indecent way, with the suffering and the precarious lives exposed in *Agent Orange*. What *Viet Nam at Peace* painfully recalls is the passing of time and the possible erasure of memory. Yet, the third volume is also probably the one that offers the most comprehensive vision of post-war Vietnam. In addition to presenting another collection of Napalm and Agent Orange victims, it shows life in the debris of war, the extreme poverty that plagues villages and cities, the 'boat people' and the survivors of the infamous My Lai massacre of March 1968. Perhaps the most shattering way to enter Griffiths's work is to read the Trilogy backwards, from the third to the first volume, to fully grasp the horror that was to come, but could only be partially made out in *Vietnam Inc.*

Works Cited

Agamben, Giorgio. *Remnants of Auschwitz: The Witness and the Archive*. New York: Zone Books, 1999.

Barthes, Roland. *La Chambre claire*. Paris: Gallimard, Le Seuil, 1980.

Brockway, Anthony. "An Interview with Philip Jones Griffiths." *Babylon Wales* May 2004. Retrieved 8 April 2013. <http://www.babylonwales.veryweird.com/>.

Dannin, Bob. "The Anarchist Journalist: Interview with Philip Jones Griffiths. New York City." *Musarium*. Jan. 2002. Retrieved 8 May 2012. <http://www.musarium.com/stories/vietnaminc/moviehtml/movieanarchists.html>.

—. "Choking Photograph: Interview with Philip Jones Griffiths. New York City." *Musarium*. Jan. 2002. Retrieved 8 May 2012. <http://www.musarium.com/stories/vietnaminc/moviehtml/choking-photo.html>.

Didi-Huberman, Georges. *Images in Spite of All: Four Photographs from Auschwitz*. Chicago, IL: The University of Chicago Press, 2008. [French original: *Images malgré tout*. Paris: Editions de Minuit, 2003].

Griffiths, Philip Jones. *Agent Orange: "Collateral Damage" in Viet Nam*. London: Trolley, 2003.

—. "Introduction. Agent Orange: 'Collateral Damage' in Viet Nam." *The Digital Journalist*. Jan. 2003. Retrieved 2 May 2012. <http://digitaljournalist.org/issue0401/griffiths.html>.

—. *Viet Nam at Peace*. London: Trolley, 2005.

—. *Vietnam Inc. 1971*. London: Phaidon Press, 2001.

Harrison, Graham. "Philip Jones Griffiths: Interview by Graham Harrison." *Photo Histories*. June 2007. Retrieved 6 May 2012. <http://www.photohistories.com/interviews/23/philip-jones-griffiths?pg=all>.

Howe, Peter. "The Dauntless Spirit Philip Jones Griffiths: 1936-2008." *The Digital Journalist*. April 2008. Retrieved 8 May 2012. <http://digitaljournalist.org/issue0804/the-dauntless-spirit-philip-jones-griffiths-1936-2008.html>.

Kempf, Jean. "Qu'est-ce qu'un regard photographique? Garry Winogrand au fil du rasoir." *Cercles* 2 (1992): 169-177. Avaliable online at HAL. 14 May 2009. Retrieved 19 May 2012. <http://halshs.archives-ouvertes.fr/halshs-00382258/fr/>.

Lauzon, Jean. *La Photographie malgré l'image*. Ottawa: Les Presses de l'Université d'Ottawa, 2002.

"Philip Jones Griffiths Discussing Agent Orange: "Collateral Damage" in Viet Nam." Interview. Video clip. *The Digital Journalist*. Jan. 2003. Retrieved 8 May 2012. <http://digitaljournalist.org/issue0401/video/griffiths13.mov>.

Sontag, Susan. *On Photography*. 1977. New York: Anchor Books, 1990.

—. *Regarding the Pain of Others*. New York: Picador, 2004.

Taylor, John. *Body Horror: Photojournalism, Catastrophe and War*. Manchester: Manchester University Press, 1998.

Rudolph Glitz

Facing the Feral Child: Precarious Futures in Three Popular Science-Fiction Narratives

1. Precariousness and the Child

The following discussion of George Miller's film *The Road Warrior* (1981) from the *Mad Max* series, James Cameron's *Aliens* (1986) and the computer game *BioShock* (2007) will take for granted the cultural significance of these relatively recent and still widely popular science-fiction narratives as well as their representativeness as instantiations of the feral child trope. It aims not only to shed some new light on the political and moral implications of the three narratives themselves, but also to contribute to the closely inter-related debates surrounding, on the one hand, the trope of the child more generally and, on the other, the condition of precariousness and its representation. More specifically, the three narratives will be read through pertinent sections of, firstly, Judith Butler's acclaimed *Precarious Life* of 2004 and, secondly, Lee Edelman's in some ways similar and perhaps similarly influential study *No Future* of the same year. After each of these readings, I will invert the hierarchy that is inevitably established by reading artefacts in terms of theoretical texts by highlighting the considerable challenges which the three narratives pose, in turn, to Edelman's and Butler's arguments – challenges that, in their abstract form, deserve more careful consideration than the two theorists give them, and which also happen to inform my own interpretive position.

The child as embodiment of precariousness is a figure quite familiar to us from the visual and literary arts, where it mobilizes our moral intuitions in such diverse canonical contexts as Homer's *Iliad*, Shakespeare's *Richard III*, David's painting *Little Drummer Boy* (or *Mort de Joseph Bara*), Andersen's "Little Match Girl", a whole range of literary classics by Dickens, or Picasso's *Boy with a Dog*. At least since Rousseau's celebration of children's noble because still savage and uncorrupted humanity, the figure of the child has also become increasingly present in non-fictional, or semi-fictional, forms of public discourse. Most notably in the field of politics, children are regularly enlisted to represent the vulnerability and endangered future of whichever imagined community the audience is meant to identify with – that of the nation, for example, in debates about state-funded education,[1] or of mankind as a whole in such global humanist endeavours as the fight against world hunger.[2] Occasionally, we might find representations of vulnerable youngsters put to use in more aggressively discriminatory propaganda, such as the eugenicist fear-mongering of the Third Reich, in which children with visible birth

[1] Cf., for instance, the American "No Child Left Behind" policy.
[2] Cf. almost any campaign poster involved in that project.

defects were displayed to muster support for the state's euthanasia programmes (cf. US Holocaust Memorial Museum). However, children's comparative lack of social allegiances and power, their physiognomic similarities across cultures and gene pools, and their near-universal appeal to the adult's protective instincts all tend to work against such exclusionary usages, and in fact have made the humanist interpretation of the vulnerable child figure something of a default reading. It is certainly used as such by the creators of many politically informed science-fiction narratives, whose more prominent child characters serve to represent the precariousness of our human condition over and above any more localized concerns.

Very often in such narratives, the humanist dimension of the child figure is additionally reinforced by the employment of a particular subtype of the trope, namely that of the feral child. The first codifications of the feral child figure in this broad representative function can be traced back to the *ancien régime*, Linnaean biology and the Enlightenment tradition of the noble savage that also influenced Rousseau, but its history and semantic charge is at least equally infused by now with the Darwinian view of nature as a site of permanent struggle and adaptation. As a Western reader, and depending on one's cultural background, one's first immediate associations with feral children may be with the story of the German foundling Kaspar Hauser, Kipling's Mowgli from *The Jungle Book* or young Victor from Truffaut's *L'enfant sauvage*. Yet science-fiction fans are just as likely to recall the nameless feral boy from the second instalment of Mel Gibson's *Mad Max* series, or the traumatized "Newt", as she calls herself, from James Cameron's celebrated sequel to *Alien*. Furthermore, media consumers familiar with both science fiction and recent computer game culture might even recall the so-called "little sisters" from the bestselling *BioShock* franchise, i.e. a tribe of cartoonish Alice-in-Wonderland look-alikes who may be less hairy and better-dressed than their cinematic counterparts, but are certainly no less wildly behaved.

Yet how exactly does the figure of the feral child fit into the narratives in question? In the case of Miller's *The Road Warrior*, the unnamed boy's ferocity and inarticulateness are clearly products of the dystopian Australian wastelands around him, an environment where the struggle for scarce resources has reduced all manifestations of humanizing culture to a minimum and is threatening to cast *homo sapiens* back into a state of sheer animality. Correspondingly, the happy ending of the narrative, i.e. the lasting redemption of the human community thanks to their champion, the Road Warrior, is signalled by the feral boy revealing himself as the speaker of the film's voice-over. In other words, the threat of dehumanization is shown to have been lastingly averted by the film pointing us to the little boy's eventual transition from grunting *enfant sauvage* to social being *par excellence* and authoritative wielder of language.

In Cameron's *Aliens*, the threat to humanity as represented by the feral child is fundamentally similar although the details are different. Newt is discovered by the heroine Ripley and accompanying soldiers as the only survivor of an alien-infested colony in outer space. During months of eluding the aliens, she has shed all marks of her acculturation and learnt to behave more like a frightened rodent than a human being, thus providing Ripley as well as the cinema audience with a glum forecast of humanity's fate in case the aliens ever make it to earth. In the course of the film, with the aliens being gradually fought back, the wild and withdrawn Newt turns into a more conventional little girl again. At the end, after Ripley has once again kept mankind safe from its alien predator, Newt trustingly allows herself to be taken to hyper-sleep by her new surrogate mother.

BioShock, finally, places its feral children in the setting of a crumbling dystopian underwater society built on the laissez-faire philosophy of the writer Ayn Rand. Through drugs, psychological conditioning and implants, the orphan girls called "little sisters" in the game have been turned into delusional scavengers whose sole aim it is to extract a valuable serum called ADAM from the corpses scattered across the city. Yet here, too, the feral child figure represents more than merely its particular social role and ludic function in the game world. She also figures prominently in the final cutscenes that mark the various available end points of the interactive game narrative. Depending on how the player character treats the little sisters during game play, they will end up either as a pack of murderous cut-throats let loose upon a surface world threatened by nuclear disaster and anarchy, or as educated, happily married mothers, in whose picket-fenced suburban family circle the player character lives out his subsequent life.

Evidently, then, all three narratives use the figure of the child metonymically in order to represent the precarious future of humanity. By representing feral children, furthermore, they indicate a concern with more than just biological survival. The precariousness in question is not merely that of the species of *homo sapiens*, but extends, quite crucially, to its civilizational achievements and legacy. In each case, the plot of the narrative moves not only towards ensuring the child's continued survival, but also towards ensuring its extraction from a purely Darwinian struggle for survival and reintegration into civilized society. Insofar as the latter involves the imposition of certain norms and conventions, it renders the three narratives political and lays them open to critiques such as Butler's and Edelman's.

2. The Feral Child as Embodiment of the Face

In *Precarious Life*, Judith Butler considers the "face" as primarily a pre-linguistic appeal addressed to us by the precarious presence of the human other. The face is an appeal, more precisely, that awakens us to the precariousness of the other, which in itself constitutes a primary and irreducible experience, and forms the essence of our morality. Our awakeness to the precariousness of the other in turn takes the form of a struggle. As Levinas puts it in "Peace and Proximity": "the face of the other in its precariousness and defencelessness, is for me at once the temptation to kill and the call to peace, the 'You shall not kill'" (qtd. in Butler, 134). And as Butler further explicates: "If the Other, the Other's face, which, after all, carries the meaning of this precariousness, at once tempts me with murder and prohibits me from acting upon it, then the face operates to produce a struggle for me, and establishes this struggle at the heart of ethics" (135). It is important to note here that the struggle in question is by no means one we should be keen to avoid or end in Butler's and Levinas's view. On the contrary, the struggle is welcomed by them as a state of tension whose unresolved maintenance is crucial for any peaceful and non-violent encounter with the other to take place.

Keeping this in mind, we can turn to the feral children in our three narratives and ask whether they could possibly be seen as engaging the protagonists of their respective narratives and, through them, their audiences, in such peace-producing face-to-face encounters as Butler envisages. In the first meeting between Mad Max and the feral boy, who has just used his razor-sharp boomerang to kill a man and chop off another one's fingers, the tension between murderous aversion and anxiousness not to kill seems at least momentarily established. As the camera switches back and forth between their faces, Max's stoically motionless features remain inscrutable and his initial attitude towards the child uncertain. Together with the fact that the subsequent relationship between the two remains entirely non-verbal and hard to distinguish from mere tolerance of one another's presence, this uncertainty lends at least some credence to the notion that we might be dealing with a fictional instantiation of the face.

Newt's case is more difficult to construe along these lines since her feral condition is less deeply marked and thus the threat of her otherness less firmly established. However, when first encountering her, the trigger-happy marines that accompany Ripley promptly mistake her for an alien and fire in her direction. It takes Ripley's intervention to stop them and induce the child to communicate by means of patient listening, sympathetic face-to-face glances and touches. Although Ripley is clearly not struggling with the temptation to kill the girl at this or, in fact, any point in the narrative, one could still read the film as having externalized the Levinasian struggle by attributing the murderous impulse in question to the soldiers and the interdiction against it to Ripley, and thus having conveyed at least a hint of the Levinasian face in action.

The encounter with the little sisters in *BioShock*, finally, contains numerous striking similarities with Butler's account. The ethical component of the game that made it notorious and caused some media outrage when it came out (cf. Gross) consists precisely of the player character coming face-to-face with the little sisters and having to fight an internal struggle. For whenever the (male) avatar gets hold of a sister, the player is required to choose between a) the option of killing her and harvesting her serum by ripping out her implant, or b) curing her of her delusional, feral state and selflessly foregoing the additional power boost granted by her death, albeit for at least partial compensation later in the game. If this moment of deciding between whether to kill or not to kill the fearful and manifestly vulnerable little girl does not constitute a fictional encounter with Butler's face, one might wonder what does.

However, persuasive as these assessments may appear at first sight, they are still incomplete since they have not yet taken into account Butler's rather peculiar attitude towards representation. Throughout her entire chapter on the face, Butler seems extremely suspicious of our image-forming practices and primarily associates representation with the dehumanization and obliteration of the other. Thus, she argues with Levinas that "some loss of the human takes place when it is 'captured' by the image" (145), and in fact describes representation as incompatible with encountering the face except in the few cases when it "not only fails to capture its referent but *shows* its failing" (146), i.e. in cases where it does not diminish our exposure to the precarious other and the concomitant tension it produces. This does not bode well for the three science-fiction narratives we are investigating.

In the first one, the lasting peace and possible friendship between Mad Max and the boy seems to a large extent based on the resolution of the primary struggle Butler outlines – a resolution, furthermore, that is achieved through representation. For as viewers of the film may remember, Max eventually resolves his presumed internal struggle between wanting to kill the feral child and shying away from such a deed by throwing him a hurdy gurdy. Only after the boy laughs and plays with this musical toy, whose tune, significantly, is that of "Happy Birthday", does Max categorize him as a little *homo ludens* rather than a dangerous and aggressive animal that invites extermination. In *Aliens*, too, one can find clear signs that representational categories are at work in the heroine's encounter with Newt. Ripley's image of the orphan girl takes its cue from an old school photograph that shows Newt as the golden-haired winner of a spelling contest, and is further informed by the loss of her own daughter, whose role the girl is increasingly shown to fill as the film progresses. Refraining from killing the little sisters in *BioShock*, finally, is not the result of continued tension and un-resolve on the part of the player – the game is on hold during the decision-making process – but coincides with his preferring one representation of the girls that is offered by the game to another, namely that which frames them as human and innocent victims of abuse over that which frames them as inhuman monsters whose survival poses a threat.

By thus invariably relying on what must be regarded as representational paradigms of the human, all three of our fictional examples actually show the dehumanization of the feral child in Butler's somewhat paradoxical sense of the word – paradoxical because the act of classifying someone as human is usually regarded as humanizing them rather than the opposite. Due to their dehumanizing effect in the Butlerian sense, the three science-fictional encounters with the child are not, after all, presenting us with the face proper. This is because, according to Butler and Levinas, the face proper is markedly opposed to any paradigms of the human, as becomes obvious when Butler asks: "Do we encounter those faces in the Levinasian sense, or are these, in various ways, images that, through their frame, produce the paradigmatically human, become the very cultural means through which the paradigmatically human is established?" (143). As far as the feral children in our science-fiction narratives are concerned, our answer would evidently have to be the second.

It is true, of course, that the paradigms of the human produced by the three science-fiction narratives can be seen as conventional to the point of oppressiveness. The *homo ludens* and later political leader and storyteller in *The Road Warrior*, the sweet, pretty and frightened daughter in distress in *Aliens*, and the middle-class student, wife, mother and care-giver in *BioShock* are all ideals that can easily be politically instrumentalized, and this may well be to the detriment of alternative life-course models. Yet one might still regard these paradigms as posing a challenge to Butler's account. After all, such political instrumentalization is neither inevitable nor irresistible, and unlike the often 9/11-related examples Butler adduces in her text, the representational resolutions of the primary moral struggle she envisages do not, in our three narratives, result in actual death and suffering. If the protagonists of these narratives 'kill' the other of the feral child by fixing it "in a formulated phrase", to speak with T. S. Eliot's Prufrock, they do so at most metaphorically, and even on the metaphorical level terms such as "dehumanization" or "violence" seem excessive since the children are not, by such representations alone, prevented from resisting their allotted paradigms in the future and getting others to revise their conception of the human. Nor are we as consumers of these texts prevented from taking a stance against their political biases. In fact these oppressive biases seem far more likely to elicit political opposition and counter-initiatives than any face-preserving stance of non-commitment could do. Correspondingly, it would be hard to deny that by paradigmatically humanizing the children in question, by making sense of them interpretively, however reductive their interpretations might be, the heroes and heroines of the three narratives also happen to commit themselves to actively protecting and supporting them, which is something that a sustained encounter with Levinas's face does not seem capable of achieving.

3. The Feral Child as Embodiment of Reproductive Futurism

In my provisional Butlerian readings of the three science-fiction texts, I have invariably located the precarious in the figure of the feral child. I have done so in the light of a long Western tradition of representing children, namely that which tends to cast them – feral as well as non-feral – as embodiments of futurity. This tradition itself can be challenged, however, and it has been challenged to some acclaim by a self-consciously polemic contribution to the field of queer studies. Lee Edelman's book *No Future* may not explicitly address the concept of the precarious, yet by challenging widespread views of the child as inherently in need of protection and at the same time claiming for the queer a position outside the realm of representation, he still engages with both the mainstream understanding of the term and Butler's Levinasian one. Drawing primarily on right-wing pro-life slogans, but also including liberal invocations of the child figure in his attack, he warns against the universalized "fantasy subtending the image of the child" (2), the collective fantasy "in which the Child has come to embody for us the telos of the social order and come to be seen as the one for whom that order is held in perpetual trust" (11).

In Edelman's view, the logic of this fantasy – appealing though it may be to our protective instincts *vis-à-vis* the precarious – is actually oppressive. He calls it "reproductive futurism" (2), separates it from any concern with the well-being of actual children (11), and describes it as a weapon of political rhetoric aimed predominantly at the queer community:

> [T]he lives, the speech, and the freedoms of adults face constant threat of curtailment out of deference to imaginary Children whose futures [...] are construed as endangered by the social disease as which queer sexualities register. (19)

What makes reproductive futurism particularly pernicious in Edelman's view is its wide acceptance across the political spectrum. He goes as far as to describe it as inseparably intertwined with the political in general, and thus as excluding from that category any queer resistance to heteronormativity. The "fantasy of the Child", as he puts it, forces us

> to submit to the framing of political debate – and, indeed, of the political field – as defined by the terms of what this book describes as reproductive futurism: terms that impose an ideological limit on political discourse as such, preserving in the process the absolute privilege of heteronormativity by rendering unthinkable, by casting outside the political domain, the possibility of a queer resistance to this organizing principle of communal relations. (2)

While passages such as this one and most of Edelman's examples still seem to deal with a clearly delimited field of discourse – namely politics understood as mainstream American party politics – his argument soon (and not always justifiably) broadens to include language as a whole. By blithely equating his category of the political with the entirety of what Lacan has called the Symbolic (Edelman 22), he arrives at the conclusion that the queer are regarded as inimical to that order and encourages them to embrace their outcast condition. According to him, the queer is defined by, and needs to embody, "the remainder of the Real internal to the Symbolic order" (25), "the undoing of the Symbolic, and of the Symbolic subject as well" (27). This metaphysical understanding of queerness gradually replaces Edelman's initial association of queerness with sexuality and deviation from heteronormativity (17), which can be seen as his response to the problem of sexually queered identities that are manifestly operating within the symbolic order, liberal politics, and even the dictates of reproductive futurism (17). By conceiving of the queer as a *jouissance* that leads to an escape from the "paternal metaphor of the name", "from the alienation intrinsic to meaning" (25), Edelman approximates quite closely the extra-representational condition of the precarious other, whose face we have already encountered in the context of Butler's argumentation.

As popularising, if not even paradigmatic, instantiations of the "fantasy of the Child", *The Road Warrior*, *Aliens* and *BioShock* would all be expected to confirm Edelman's observations. But do they? And, if yes, to what extent and how exactly? The first notable feature of the three narratives that can be seen as supporting Edelman's claims is the fact that they all unreservedly privilege the protection of the future as embodied by their various child figures over the respective alternatives offered. In *The Road Warrior*, we are obviously invited to sympathize with the community of settlers the feral kid will eventually grow up to lead – rather than the nomadic raiders commanded by the tyrannical Humungus. In *Aliens*, we are just as obviously encouraged to side with the risk-averse and maternally protective Ripley against both the company representative who, driven by capitalist greed, tries to secure the aliens for immediate financial profit and the predatory aliens themselves. In *BioShock*, finally, even if we deliberately choose the 'bad' path, we are continually reminded of, and supposed to recognize, the moral as well as political preferability of the peaceful ending of the game over the slaughter unleashed by sacrificing the little sisters to our own selfish needs – over a scenario, more precisely, which culminates in our seizure of nuclear weaponry and world domination, yet in which the scolding narrator leaves us doubtful not only about everyone else's personal happiness but also our own.

Secondly, Edelman's claim about the limitation of the category of the political to models of society that endorse reproductive futurism gains at least some support from the fact that the non-future-oriented alternatives presented in the three narratives all embody, or at least herald, a breakdown of civilization as the term has been traditionally understood in Western history. Despite their motorization, the marauders in *The Road Warrior* display many stereotypical characteristics of the two primary pre-modern challengers of the so-called civilized order: the Barbarian and the primitive savage. Not only does their leader sport a masque reminiscent of a gladiator's helmet, a pseudo-Latin name and a body-builder physique that prefigures Schwarzenegger's Conan; many of his followers – in addition to their nomadism, hunting and plundering – also wear leather, fur and feather adornments that sometimes take the shape of tails. In stereotypically savage fashion, they sport Mohawk hairstyles, shoot arrows, waylay convoys and circle the fort of the settlers while uttering high-pitched yells. A victory of the marauders here would hardly make for a more stable political system than one in which Cameron's aliens were to reduce humanity to meat-providing carrier hosts before wiping them out entirely, or a thoroughly "bioshocked" planet Earth wrecked by nuclear warfare, roamed by the player's genetically mutated and deluded minions, and continuing to crumble in the grip of his regime.

Thirdly, the reproductive futurism promoted in each of the three narratives is accompanied by more or less subtle heteronormative imperatives. Significantly, these imperatives go even beyond the reproductively futurist invocation of the precarious child image itself. In the case of the *The Road Warrior*, the identification of the future-oriented civilized order with heteronormativity takes on a blatantly homophobic dimension. As Rebecca Johinke notes in her article on masculinity in the *Mad Max* series: "the fact that Max and the other 'goodies' (i.e. Goose, Gyro Captain, Pappagallo, and Curmudgeon) are heterosexual, and almost to the man the 'baddies' are homosexual, must say something about value judgements" (121-122). Even though Johinke's qualifying "almost" here applies to the settler community as well, which, at least according to the Gyro Captain, could also cater to any homosexual urges the new arrival Max might have, by and large the settlers are organized along markedly heterosexual lines and as such indeed starkly opposed to the gang of marauders, whose homosexuality is flaunted throughout the film.

Compared to *The Road Warrior*, *Aliens* is refreshingly free of direct homophobia. In fact, its portrayal of the stereotypically butch marine, Private Vasquez, elicits sympathy and respect from the viewer and is manifestly designed to do so. However, this does not rule out the workings of heteronormative imperatives. Unlike the fourth film of the *Alien* franchise, the second one is still far from acknowledging Ripley's own contemporary significance as a Lesbian icon. In fact, the introduction of a gay goody such as Vasquez may well constitute an attempt to protect the central heroine from less easily containable queering appropriations. As Jeffrey A. Brown points out:

> Due to the homophobic nature of most mainstream audiences, many narratives overtly seek to establish the heterosexuality of action heroines by providing a nominal male love interest or, as in *Aliens* and *Terminator 2*, by linking the action heroine to notions of a fierce maternal instinct. The lesbian innuendoes about the muscular/masculine woman are reserved for lesser and more expendable characters who are portrayed as butch. (62)

As it happens, even the heteronormative male love interest Brown mentions is hinted at in *Aliens*, namely in the form of Corporal Dwayne Hicks. Hicks, who is played by the same actor as Linda Hamilton's love interest in *Terminator*, shows Ripley how to handle his pulse rifle in a scene that is at least mildly erotically suggestive, and towards the end of the film he exchanges first names and meaningful glances with her before asking her not to stay away for long.

BioShock, too, does not seem particularly biased against homosexual orientations as such: in keeping with the taboos of 1950s America, during which the game's plot is supposed to unfold, homosexuality is neither particularly prominent in the general corruption of the underwater city nor entirely absent as a possibility. This is exemplified by the non-player-character Sander Cohen, a flamboyant artist and political leader whose character was inspired by Noël Coward and Salvador Dalí. Cohen is suggestively referred to as an "old fruit" by his former companions, and his insane obsession with wearing a rabbit mask might well constitute a direct reaction to the pressures of reproductive futurism (cf. "Queer Characters: *BioShock*"). Nevertheless, even the game world's historical setting cannot fully account for the cliché-ridden one-fits-all representtation of the little sisters' future life courses in the 'good' ending. These sugary animations may be short compared to the many hours of active game time, yet as teleological end points of the narrative they are bound to linger in the triumphant player's mind, and it is hard not to read them as simply equating heterosexual monogamy, an engagement ring and the joys of suburban motherhood with the pinnacle of human happiness – whether experienced directly or from the vantage point of a paternal guardian (i.e. that of the player character). Strictly speaking, of course, the game does not rule out the possibility of queer alternatives to the one-life-course model it celebrates. Yet by not even showing a glimpse of them – as it does, for instance, of inter-racial marriage by representing the anonymous husband figure with a significantly darker-skinned arm than the little sister's – it still conforms to the conventional heteronormative preference that is presumably shared by most of its buyers. Like the other two narratives, *BioShock* appears to confirm Edelman's point about the heteronormativity of reproductive futurism.

Yet are these correspondences sufficient for the three narratives to lend credibility to Edelman's claims about the radical exclusion from discourse of the precarious queer? I would argue that in spite of their conformism and heteronormative biases, they are not, but rather pose a challenge to Edelman's claims. More specifically, they challenge the view that not just reproductive futurism, but all politics and even the symbolic order as a whole can be seen as practically coterminous. While it is true, as we have seen, that anti-futurist alternatives such as those presented in the three narratives have frequently been distinguished from the political understood as civilized, this has usually been done as an act of highly politicized wishful thinking rather than systematically and in the context of (comparatively) disinterested philosophical enquiry. Building on the latter – for instance in the broad tradition of Hobbes or the Utilitarian philosophers – there are other and arguably far more influential and widely-shared conceptions of the political that readily include all three of the anti-futurist visions of humanity we encounter in our examples.

In fact, these visions are not only theoretically recognized as political, but they also have obvious analogies in our records of political practice: justly or not, the Mongolian conquest, the environmentally hazardous depletion of the world's natural resources by the industrial West, and totalitarian leader cults such as Nazism or Stalinism (especially in their final suicidal or near-suicidal stages)[3] have long been categorized as historical examples of, respectively, a parasitically destructive politics of plunder driven by sadistic and sexually dubious male hedonism (*The Road Warrior*), politically organized short-term profiteering at the cost of future generations (*Aliens*) and megalomaniacal power politics (*BioShock*). Relying, as Edelman does, on a very narrow range of examples from the American two-party system and equating current American party

[3] Cf., for instance, Oliver Hirschbiegel's film *Der Untergang* (2004).

politics with politics in general are clearly unhelpful practices when it comes to determining what can or cannot be accommodated in the political field as it is commonly understood.

Despite this objection, Edelman's wholesale identification of the political with reproductive futurism and heteronormativity would still be acceptable as a context-specific conceptual choice if he did not ignore its very context-specificity in the subsequent steps of his argument. There is no justification whatsoever for Edelman's claims that the space outside reproductive futurism, outside the framework of all politics as he understands it, is also the space of the "unthinkable" (2), and that opposing this framework under the label of queerness as defined by conservatives amounts to refusing "the logic of opposition", "every substantialization of identity", "history as a linear narrative", and in fact the entire "law of the Symbolic" in the Lacanian sense of the term (4-5). As the three science-fiction narratives show, such opposition can easily be accommodated in the symbolic order and is far from unrepresentable. Whether in the form of a marauder in the gang of the Lord Humungus, the self-centred corporate careerist in *Aliens*, the infanticidal dictator in *BioShock* or any other fictional and historical example, opposing reproductive futurism simply amounts to assuming yet another political identity in our pluralist society. The three narratives illustrate that the symbolic order is by no means co-extensive with either reproductive futurism or, by implication, heteronormativity – however widely accepted, morally favoured and excessively privileged these latter ideologies may be. Despite its inevitable biases, the symbolic order encompasses both reproductive futurism and its various anti-futurist alternatives, just as it encompasses many other sites of political contestation where one side is temporarily favoured but by no means the only one imaginable or actually in existence.

Without any special connection between reproductive futurism and the symbolic order as a whole, Edelman's conception of the precarious, anti-futurist queer is bound to crumble. Even if it were possible deliberately to follow his recommendation and take, or be seen as taking, a position outside the struggle of identity politics and the symbolic order (4), why should one regard this position as an escape from reproductive futurism rather than its opposite? Identifying, as Edelman puts it, "with the undoing of identity, which is also to say with the disarticulation of social and Symbolic form" (30) would surely mean rejecting anti-futurism just as much as reproductive futurism or any other identity constructed by language, myths and other narratives. It would lead to the same precarious limbo of non-commitment we have already seen championed by Butler, and presumably would entail similar problems.

In his demonization of representation under the label of the symbolic order, Edelman underestimates the interpretive possibilities and potential subversions of the status quo that emerge from even such relatively conformist texts as our three science-fiction narratives. While they certainly endorse reproductive futurism over the various anti-futurist alternatives on offer, the futurist societies sketched in them do not, in principle, rule out a dynamic pluralism of shifting identities that can also accommodate queer sexualities (cf. Edelman 28). Heteronormative though they all are, none of the three narratives denies the individual's right to resist, as far as his or her own life is concerned, the reproductive imperative; none of them denies his or her right not to 'go forth and multiply' and thus to oppose the imperative Edelman seems to see lurking everywhere.

On the contrary, a certain tolerance of the non-futurist position can already be inferred from the heroic status of the protagonists. The fact that Max, Ripley and the *BioShock* avatar risk their own well-being for the future as embodied by the feral child figure is not presented as a moral obligation or widely enforceable norm. Instead, the three protagonists are celebrated and commemorated as exceptional. Their reproductive futurism appears against a backdrop of more hedonistic default positions that place a higher value on the here and now.

Furthermore, there is the subversive potential of the cultural myths and inter-texts that inform the three narratives. Thus the three protagonists share at least some of their characteristics with the non-reproductively active 'lone horseman' figure from the tradition of the American Western. The biblical myth of the celibate Jesus Christ is also alluded to by each of the three saviour figures in our texts, and it points to a reservoir of potentially subversive narratives only waiting to be adapted by the social critic.[4] Edelman's narrow focus on normative parenthood has led him to overlook existing, widely accepted, and yet potentially subversive political goals that are not necessarily tied to reproduction, goals that – thanks, perhaps, to the pluralism arising from division of labour and its division of society into soldiers, saints, settlers etc. – can even be found in heteronormative or right-wing visions of society. Saintly soldiers of fortune such as Mad Max, Ripley or the *BioShock* avatar may well be conceived of as serving a society committed to reproductive futurism, but this does not mean that related subcultures such as the military or the church need to subscribe to that futurism themselves. Whether and how the occasionally apocalyptic tendencies in such subcultures could and should be mobilized, adapted or emulated to serve the cause of the queer still remains to be worked out and debated. Yet the very existence of subcultures with widely divergent value systems and the sheer variety of political and personal life-style models that relate to the future in a variety of different ways already belie the homogenizing dichotomy Edelman sets up. Provided we join the struggle of ideas and representations by way of reinterpreting, dynamically combining and modifying what we find, such plurality rather suggests genuine possibilities of change. Despite the undeniable biases of existing popular narratives and contrary to Edelman's pessimism with regard to all representational politics, these possibilities promise far more than fantasies that merely "reproduce the past" (31).

Last but by no means least, Edelman as well as Butler's mistrust of representation is effectively challenged by the inherent open-endedness of at least one particular form of it. Narrative, perhaps as opposed to more static ways of meaning production, is inherently open to revision. First of all, it regularly points beyond itself and flaunts its provisionality, for instance when Mad Max leaves the settlers at the end of *The Road Warrior* and we are left wondering about future adventures he might have as well as the long-term fate of the community he saved. Secondly, it invariably allows for future additions even in cases where the central plot line has been neatly wrapped up and the narrative has established a "sense of an ending" of the kind discussed by Frank

[4] Due to the apocalyptic expectations of the first Christians, for example, Christianity's famous injunction to procreate is countered by such lastingly influential doctrines as those of the celibate Saint Paul, who, in 1 Corinthians 7, wishes "that all were as I am" and that "those who have wives should be as though they had none".

Kermode. Thus the peaceful and heteronormatively inflected relief established at the end of *Aliens*, when the nuclear pseudo-family of Newt, Hicks and Ripley can finally enter hypersleep, is easily rendered null and void in the next instalment of the series, which shows Ricks and Newt dead and informs us that one of the xenomorphs made it onto the rescue vessel. For the precarious status of both the feral child and the queer adult who might feel oppressed by the latter's symbolism, this open-endedness of the narrative medium means that there is always a chance of corrective adjustment. No paradigm of the human or symbolic structure that is established by means of narrative is ever entirely fixed and immutable. It invariably and necessarily retains at least a minimum of responsiveness to the precarious pre-representational other, a responsiveness that can be exploited in the fight against oppression.

4. Conclusion

After reading *The Road Warrior*, *Aliens* and *BioShock* as instances of Butler's and Edelman's broader theoretical claims and in turn highlighting the challenges they pose to the latter, I have arrived at the following conclusions. Despite their undeniable heteronormativity and oppressively conventional humanism, the science-fictional representations of the feral child in these narratives do not lend unqualified support to the critiques of the two theorists. By imagining political scenarios that are at least slightly removed from the latter's immediate polemical concerns, the three narratives highlight for both Edelman and Butler a problematic wholesale rejection of "the Symbolic" or "representation" due to particular abusive instances of it. Although the full extent of this rejection is not always explicitly acknowledged – Butler, for instance, allows for an acceptable kind of representation that only represents its own failing – it still seems to guide the two theorists' lines of argumentation, which tend to downplay or omit any politically desirable counter-examples as well as the almost always available possibility of correcting at least some representational abuses. In Edelman's case, queer or queer-friendly readers are ultimately left with the question of why to exchange their intra-symbolic struggle for a society that better accommodates the queer in favour of a vaguely oppositional stance of figuring universal resistance that has no particular link to their queerness whatsoever. With regard to Butler, we are left wondering whether to accept her dismissal of even reductive representational practices in favour of an encounter with a face that leaves us hovering, Hamlet-like, in a moral and interpretive limbo, one whose paralysing effect might, in some contexts, turn out to be conducive to peace, but in others might not. Surely Edelman's rejection of the symbolic order as a whole is an exaggerated response to the oppressive nature of some of its instances. And surely Butler is throwing out undeniable benefits of abstracting and mythologizing representation with the bathwater of its exploitation by the Bushes of this world. Contrary to both, the position I would offer for consideration here and which certainly seems adequate with regard to the feral children we have looked at is this: however paradigmatic and open to discriminatory abuse it may be, representation as such is not the problem, but rather certain representations – representations that are best fought by means of other representations, whose continual creation and modification is the way in which the other makes its precarious presence felt to us.

Works Cited

BioShock. 2K Boston. 2K Games, 2007.

Brown, Jeffrey A. "Gender and the Action Heroine: Hardbodies and the Point of No Return." *Cinema Journal* 35.3 (1996): 52-71.

Butler, Judith. *Precarious Life: The Powers of Mourning and Violence*. London: Verso, 2004.

Aliens. Dir. James Cameron. Twentieth Century Fox, 1986.

Edelman, Lee. *No Future: Queer Theory and the Death Drive*. Durham, NC: Duke University Press, 2004.

Gross, Doug. "The 10 Biggest Violent Video-Game Controversies." *CNN: International Edition.* 29 June 2011. Retrieved 1 Nov. 2013. <http://edition.cnn.com/2011/TECH/gaming.gadgets/06/29/violent.video.games/>.

Johinke, Rebecca. "Manifestations of Masculinities: Mad Max and the Lure of the Forbidden Zone." *Journal of Australian Studies* 25.67 (2001): 118-125.

Kermode, Frank. *The Sense of an Ending: Studies in the Theory of Fiction (with a New Epilogue).* 1966. Oxford: Oxford University Press, 2000.

The Road Warrior. Dir. George Miller. Warner Bros., 1981.

"Queer Characters: *BioShock*." *Gaygamer.net*. 24 March 2011. Retrieved 30 July 2013. <http://gaygamer.net/2011/03/queer_characters_bioshock.html>.

United States Holocaust Memorial Museum. "The Holocaust." *Holocaust Encyclopedia.* Retrieved July 30 2013. <http://www.ushmm.org/wlc/en/media_ph.php?ModuleId=10005149&MediaId=1068>.

Stephanie Hoppeler and Gabriele Rippl

Narrating Radioactivity: Representations of Nuclear Disasters and Precarious Lives in Comic Books and Graphic Novels

1. Introduction: Radioactivity, Precariousness and Intermedial Narration

As Hiroshima and, more recently, Fukushima attest, radioactivity and nuclear disaster create precarious lives. Our specific focus is on how such lives are depicted in comic books and graphic novels, i.e. intermedial forms of storytelling that, contrary to comic strips, often deal with devastating experiences. Apart from nuclear disasters, comic books and graphic novels have dealt with the apocalypse, war, the Holocaust (Art Spiegelman's *Maus*), the terror of totalitarian regimes (Marjane Satrapi's *Persepolis*) and domestic, individual, as well as collective forms of violence and trauma (Neil Gaiman's *Sandman* series).[1] While comic books and graphic novels are popular intermedial art forms involving two media, text and picture, the majority of critics agree that their storytelling depends first and foremost on pictures (Rippl and Etter). There are graphic novels without text, but none without images. As such, comic books and graphic novels, like most comics, are capable of conveying things that could not be conveyed in a similar way by text alone, and it is here that their special suitability for narrating threatened and fractured lives appears to be rooted.

Before concentrating on our primary examples, it is first helpful to present some theses regarding the representation of nuclear disasters and precarious lives in comic books and graphic narratives:

1) As Ferenc Morton Szasz and others have shown, comics have played a major role in informing the American people about the advantages and disadvantages of radioactivity and nuclear power as well as "the long-term significance of the fissioned atom" since the 1930s and more especially since the 1950s: "With circulation figures reaching

[1] The term 'graphic novel' was coined by Richard Kyle in 1964 (Withrow and Danner 14) and popularized by Will Eisner, who used it to promote his 1979 book-length work *A Contract with God and Other Tenement Stories: A Graphic Novel*. When we use the term, we follow Roger Sabin's widely accepted definition that reads "any book-length comics narrative or compendium of such narratives (excepting volumes reprinting newspaper strips [...])" (4). As such, they may constitute a collection of previously serialized comic books, which we also draw on. Unlike the comic book, which conventionally uses inexpensive paper, is stapled rather than glue-bound, employs simple coloring techniques and contains advertisements but usually no original sketches, the graphic novel has a distinct appearance: glossy paper, high-quality printing, often hard-cover binding, enhanced coloring and additional material provided by the creative team, and this, along with the generic term 'novel', lends it the symbolic capital of traditional highbrow novels.

into the millions, cartoonists played a major role in forging the nation's atomic awareness for over three generations" (Szasz 1-2).

2) Comic books and graphic novels present radioactivity in two diverging ways: as daunting apocalypse which leads to devastating experiences for humans and animals, or as an exciting re-/negotiation of limits, as kicks protagonists get out of their total power over others, which usually leads to destruction on a large scale.

3) The popularity of comic book and graphic novel protagonists, who are often presented as superheroes, is not only based on the accidental discovery of radioactivity and the life-threatening nuclear disaster that ensues. It is also based on the struggle and ambivalence that many radioactively altered characters exhibit, a feature particularly evident from the early 1960s.

4) The effects of radioactivity can result in the depiction of either supercharged bodies of superheroes or of cancerous bodies of dying humans. Both options are present in our culture's collective or "social imaginary" which – according to Charles Taylor – is shaped by literature, images and other forms of cultural production.[2] Since comic books and graphic novels are global genres and attract global audiences, they have a worldwide significance and impact on collective imaginaries.

5) Graphic novels covering nuclear disaster help us to envisage a global world and to negotiate what it means to be interconnected with far away regions and people. They negotiate late modern intersections between regionalism and the global, i.e. "interconnections of global processes and events with local places and personal forms of experience" (Zapf, "Literary Ecology" 862).

6) Precarious life and human suffering after nuclear disaster challenge representation and narrative modes.[3] In *The Body in Pain* Elaine Scarry has demonstrated how physical pain caused by torture destroys language; intense pain circumvents language, it cannot be expressed verbally in a direct way. We claim that this is also true for nuclear disasters: it is not possible to narrate the unrepresentable; one can merely describe the weapon or the wound. In the case of radioactivity and nuclear disaster the problem is even more aggravated, since the most serious consequences of nuclear disasters remain "eerily invisible to the senses" (Heise 178) – the effects of a fallout cannot be immediately smelled, heard or felt. In order to learn about the initially imperceptible effects of nuclear disasters and fallout people are forced to rely on the mediation "through government institutions, corporations, news media and cultural attitudes" (Heise 179-180; cf. also Beck). According to Ursula Heise, who has worked on the Chernobyl fiction of Christa Wolf and Gabriele Wohmann,[4] "such regional and global risk scenarios challenge conventional language as well as commonsense reasoning", and hence "addressing the question involves narrative strategy as much as content" (182).

[2] According to Taylor, the social imaginary is "carried in images, stories, and legends". He defines it as "the ways people imagine their social existence, how they fit together with others, how things go on between them and their fellows, the expectations that are normally met, and the deeper normative notions and images that underlie these expectations" (23).

[3] Cf. Berger's *After the End* for a discussion of representations of post-apocalypse.

[4] Christa Wolf, *Störfall: Nachrichten eines Tages* (1987; translated into English as *Accident: A Day's News*) and Gabriele Wohmann, *Der Flötenton* (1987).

7) Comic books and graphic novels are first and foremost based on pictures which carry a large part of the narrative. It is this feature that is pivotal in the process of augmenting and enriching emotions in the recipient. Our hypothesis is that medium specificity needs to be taken into account and by their use of pictures, intermedial forms of storytelling such as comic books and graphic novels reach recipients in different ways than texts consisting exclusively of black letters on white paper. Pictures (and depictions of facial expression and bodily postures in particular) are "fast tracks to narrative empathy" (Keen, "Fast Tracks" 135) because "they convey emotional states", and thus such depictions "call[] upon readers' neural systems for recognition of basic emotions" (Keen, "Fast Tracks" 137).[5] Through visual codes and color symbolism (McCloud 118-137, 185-192) they are able to enhance the readers' participation and to express trauma, fears and anxieties.

It is important to point out that there has not yet been sufficient (empirical) research into how exactly the combination of text and pictures in comic books and graphic novels triggers emotions and empathy in recipients, and whether intermedial modes of storytelling are emotionally enhanced ways of narration which produce more intensive responses in their readers than exclusively verbal storytelling (Keen, "Fast Track" 152-153). Due to the fact that pictures are processed in the right hemisphere of the human brain, which also control emotions, psychologists and narratologists have claimed that pictures trigger more attention and emotions in recipients (the emotional impact increases with the iconicity of the pictures) and are more memorable than stories mediated via printed letters only (Nöth 467-477, 481). However, questions relating to the interrelationship between pictures and the creation of emotions can only be answered by further quantitative and qualitative research which, as Arvid Kappas and Marion G. Müller have recently suggested, requires collaboration between psychologists of emotion, visual communication researchers and visual culture experts (3-23).

8) Since comic books and graphic novels often participate in counter-discourses and follow cultural-critical impulses, they remind us of past catastrophes and warn us of possible future ones. Like literature in general, comic books and graphic novels have social implications and are a means of political participation: they are "a sensorium for the deficits and imbalances of the larger culture" (Zapf, "The State of Ecocriticism" 49); they fathom latent and displaced individual and collective fears and anxieties and allow us to deal with them in a playful way. Comic books and graphic novels enable us to experiment and try out things in our imagination; they stimulate us to imagine possible alternative worlds and to identify with others. Mass-marketed superhero comic books and graphic novels

> can provide rich aesthetic and ethical experiences. The narratives presented [...] allow readers to exercise their imaginative capacities, to contemplate contrasts between good and evil, to think about prejudice and the sociocultural nature of the self (issues nearly all superheroes face), and perhaps, to an even greater extent than the novel, to engage in emphatic exploration of the minds of others. (Pratt 103)

[5] For a discussion of the creation of empathy in novels cf. Keen (*Empathy*).

With these theses in mind, we will now turn to a discussion of radioactivity in US-American and British comic books and graphic novels published between the 1960s and the 1980s and again in the twenty-first century, which invite a global audience to ruminate on the impact of increasingly uncontrollable and dangerous military and scientific technology such as nuclear bombs and radioactivity. However, narrating nuclear risk scenarios in comic books and graphic novels has many facets, and one can also distinguish several phases that correspond to changing attitudes towards radioactivity.

2. The Advent of the Radioactively Powered Superhero: 1960s to 1970s

With the American Manhattan Project of the mid-1940s and the dropping of the atomic bombs on Japan at the end of World War II, the enormous efficacy of nuclear weapons was demonstrated to the whole world. There was an awareness of the irrefutable advantage of radioactive materials for energy production[6] and warfare on the one hand, and a tendency to ignore their problematic effects (such as disastrous radiation accidents and the disposal of nuclear waste) on the other. The late 1950s and early 1960s were a time of general social upheaval and reorientation as well as the Cold War, with the USA and the Soviet Union coming to the brink of nuclear war in 1962. Nevil Shute's 1957 novel *On the Beach* about a nuclear war and the subsequent impending extinction of all life on earth testifies to the anxieties characteristic of the time. Radioactivity was exhilarating, but also extremely frightening. This ambivalence was addressed in comic books, especially in those published by Marvel, from the 1960s. The new kinds of superheroes now appearing on the comic book stage – The Fantastic Four, Spider-Man, The Hulk, etc. – frequently had their powers bestowed on them inadvertently and more often than not experienced conflicting emotions towards them; unlike their predecessors of the late 1930s to the early 1960s – Superman, Batman, Wonder Woman, etc. – who were born as superpowered beings and employed their abilities self-assertively and benevolently.[7] This new breed of superhero was no longer confident but plagued by

[6] Reactor Chicago Pile-1, declared a National Historic Landmark in 1965, had been activated in 1942. Szasz points out that during this era, "corporations such as General Electric Company also produced a number of nonfiction comic books that urged Americans to whole-heartedly adopt nuclear power. Simultaneously, Superman's major rival Captain Marvel provided a multifaceted cartoon critique of all aspects of the fissioned atom. For about six years, Captain Marvel stories served as picture-and-text parables of the dangers that might flow from the release of atomic energy" (5).

[7] This hitherto successful superhero is commonly referred to as the Golden Age superhero. Comic book ages are sometimes divided into Golden, Silver, Bronze, Revisionist and Digital Age. In June 1939 Superman heralded the Golden Age which is generally agreed to have lasted until the reboot of the Flash in 1956. This signified the beginning of the Silver Age, which was characterized by its numerous reboots as well as the fact that origin stories and superheroes' powers tended to have scientific rather than magical roots (Cowsill et al. 80). The Bronze Age lasted roughly from the 1970s until the mid-1980s and saw the rise of darker characters and more socially relevant plot lines. The Revisionist Age, launched by such works as Alan Moore and Dave Gibbons' *Watchmen* brought even more corrosive re-examination of established notions. It was superseded around the year 2000 by the Digital Age. This final category is dis-

self-doubt and struggled with ambiguous emotions towards their newly acquired powers. At times these were cursed and concealed, at times flaunted, which is highly reminiscent of the attitude of the public towards radioactivity.

That "[t]he core formula of a scientist becoming infected or wounded by some cutting-edge research became the basis for a slew of new heroic characters" (Petersen 163) is illustrated by the many new Marvel heroes. For example, in 1961 Stan Lee and Jack Kirby launched the Fantastic Four (*Fantastic Four* #1), who were exposed to cosmic rays during a scientific mission gone awry in outer space. But the acquisition of superpowers through radioactivity was not the only novel element in these characters. Much more striking was that they digressed from the path taken by the self-assertive and confident superheroes of the preceding decades. The Fantastic Four balked at their newly found powers and only reluctantly adopted their roles as superheroes. Yet even as they came to accept the results of the radiation accident, they constantly challenged their role as superheroes. While all but Ben Grimm, who has been transformed into the monstrous 'Thing', would have been able to devise an alter ego and thereby escape the media, the Fantastic Four chose not to. As a consequence, their private and public personas were indistinguishable and often led to conflict between them.

In a variation of the *Dr Jekyll and Mr Hyde* narrative, good-natured Dr Bruce Banner was sporadically converted into the Hulk, a huge, green or gray, angry monster, following the accidental exposure to the explosion of a gamma bomb in 1962 (*The Incredible Hulk* #1). Every time Dr Banner was subjected to fear, excitement, anger or grief, his inner fiend was unleashed and wreaked havoc due to his uncontrollable strength and impulsive behavior. The Hulk was not an evil creature in himself but had difficulty in suppressing his emotions, which usually resulted in mayhem. It also triggered a form of self-loathing since Dr Banner was a vessel for diametrically opposed personae. Identifying with the shy and quiet Dr Banner made it impossible to understand the emotional and raging Hulk, and vice versa. Whereas the superheroes of the 1940s and 1950s were usually at peace with their alter ego, not only accepting but even cherishing it, Dr Banner/the Hulk is characteristic of the new kind of superhero of the 1960s whose powers were seriously detrimental to their quality of life. Likewise Spider-Man, who made his debut in 1962 (*Amazing Fantasy* #15): nerdy Peter Parker led a quiet, almost isolated existence until he was bestowed with superhuman powers from the bite of a radioactive spider. Failing to understand his new powers, Peter attempted to hide them. Only slowly did he start accepting his uniqueness, although he never completely – in the manner of Superman, for instance – stopped doubting himself and his deeds. He eventually realized that great power came with great responsibility and thus took the decision to fight evil on behalf of humanity. There are other comic book narratives that follow this new formula: a mild-mannered and likable person is accidentally exposed to radiation and, as a result, is invested with superpowers that complicate his or her life. Larry Trainor became Negative Man in 1963 (*My Greatest Adventures* #80) after he flew into a cloud of radioactive space rays, and Matthew Michael Murdoch

tinguished by the ceaseless adaptation of comic book substance into various media and a new attitude toward comic book continuity (i.e. the more or less closed narrative cosmos encompassing most of a publisher's releases) (cf. Hoppeler; Hoppeler and Rippl; Levitz).

turned into Daredevil in 1964 (*Daredevil* #1) as a consequence of being blinded in an accident involving radioactive chemicals.

While all of these new superheroes were individuals, as fans would argue, they functioned exclusively according to the core formula of "troubled characters ambivalent about their powers" (Sabin 49). To Robert P. Petersen, "[w]hat made this formula so successful was that in each instance, the transformation of the ordinary person into a superhero established a wounded character who was riddled with self-doubt as the powers bestowed upon him or her were at best a mixed blessing, both elevating and alienating him or her from ordinary life" (163). In the face of Cold War nuclear threat, the large young comic book readership – taking into account that more than fifty percent of the US population was then under the age of thirty (Boyer et al. 626) – could easily relate to the struggle of the new heroes. This explains why the period from 1961 to 1964 generated such a large number of similar characters.

In the 1970s Leonard Rifas was one of "the foremost American anti-nuclear comic book writer/publisher/distributor", who helped to distribute a number of international anti-nuclear comics such as *Atomic Horror Comic* (1977), the Canadian *Nuclear Dragons Attack* (1978)[8] and *Rumbles!* (1981) (Szasz 100).[9] More comic books and graphic novels were about to be created which were set in the middle of nuclear holocausts or their aftermath (Szasz 115-132), trying to regenerate awe for nuclear power and to offer people "a new way to comprehend the incomprehensible" (Szasz 133).

3. Depicting Worlds before and after Radioactive Disaster: The 1980s

Two graphic novels of the 1980s, Alan Moore and David Lloyd's *V for Vendetta* (released in ten monthly installments from 1982-1989) and Alan Moore and Dave Gibbons's *Watchmen* (serialized in twelve monthly installments in 1986/1987) reached their audiences in an age characterized by volatility and instability. In the US in particular unemployment rates soared, exports plummeted, divorce and abortion figures increased while the sexual revolution and women's movement caused many an American to call for restoration of traditional values (Boyer et al. 659). Both graphic novels are significant examples of how popular culture reacted to the events of the Cold War era with its anti-Soviet jargon, its military buildup and nuclear threat, which also abounded during the Reagan presidency causing millions of Americans (as well as readers elsewhere in the Western world) to feel an increase in the threat of nuclear war during the early 1980s (Boyer et al. 663).

In the midst of this uncertain and perilous backcloth, *V for Vendetta* depicts a parallel world in a United Kingdom of the near future, following a nuclear holocaust. It is strongly reminiscent of other tales of totalitarian regimes in the tradition of Ray Bradbury, Aldous Huxley and George Orwell. Radioactive catastrophe is the bedrock on which Moore and Lloyd's Cold War narrative is based; it serves as the blueprint that makes us suspend our disbelief of the rise of a dictatorial party in the UK of the 1980s.

[8] Cf. also Richard Comely's comic book *Captain Canuck* (1975), whose Canadian superhero fights evildoers's use of radioactive power.

[9] Cf. also Rifas, "Cold War Comics" and "Cartooning and Nuclear Power".

The aftermath of the nuclear war is flood, failed harvests and complete political instability. Norsefire, a fascist organization which suppresses and terrorizes citizens, has eliminated all those opposed to it in concentration camps. The protagonist V is a rebellious anarchist wearing a Guy Fawkes mask who leads the revolution. Having the young Evey by his side, V eventually succeeds in overthrowing the government.

Even more remarkable in terms of a radioactively powered superhero is the award-winning *Watchmen*. It tells a tale that mirrors life in the US in the 1980s: the moral climate is grim, people are either instrumental in the perceived decline of American culture or they are demoralized by an escalating arms spiral between East and West and their mutual terror of each other. In the fictional world of *Watchmen* an accident involving a nuclear physics experiment turns the scientist Jon Osterman into the omnipotent Dr Manhattan. The reader is introduced to his perception of the world around him and his successive estrangement through internal focalization: "The morality of my activities escapes me" (*Watchmen* VI, 14/2). Because Dr Manhattan was "made up of controlled energy in human form, it was decided he should slightly affect his surroundings by casting a soft blue light a limited distance from his presence" (Gibbons, Kidd and Essl n.p.). The bluish glow triggers associations with power and luminosity, both elements of the radioactive materials that caused the transformation of Dr Manhattan in the first place. In the guise of Dr Manhattan, the USA are finally in possession of the ultimate weapon and need no longer dread the Soviet Union, but tension builds up again when Dr Manhattan vanishes. Following a string of events, a nuclear bomb detonates in New York City taking the lives of millions of people. Both the US and the Soviet Union assume this to be the work of Dr Manhattan and feel obliged to assume peace negotiations to avoid further destruction. In truth, the devastating damage bears the signature of Ozymandias, the mastermind vigilante. He killed millions in order to rescue billions. The few who witnessed his plot carry the burden of enlightenment: "morally, you're in checkmate" (*Watchmen* XII, 20/3) as revelation would jeopardize the high price of peace.

As touched upon earlier, visual elements such as color can intensify emotional investment in that they trigger certain associations. Thus, the gloomy atmosphere of *Watchmen*, based on the unhappy tale of personal mishap, alienation, degeneracy, nuclear disaster and, finally, genocide, is accentuated by the color scheme used by John Higgins, the colorist. By choosing mainly secondary colors in a reduced color palette, he managed to invest *Watchmen* with a visual style that not only helped to create its omnipresent dismal mood but also differed from other comics of that time. Chapter VI, for instance, which is titled "The Abyss Gazes Also" after a Nietzsche quote, focuses on one of the masked vigilantes. As the bleak tale of Rorschach's childhood and young adulthood unfolds, the colors grow increasingly darker, so that the chapter ends with a panel that is entirely black. The persistent darkening of the color scheme reinforces both the narrative's and the character's turn towards the "abyss" and thus sustains a reading of a world that is approaching Armageddon.

Radioactivity plays a major role in *Watchmen* as it is (a) the source of Dr Manhattan's power and (b) the basis of the bomb that devastates New York City but then reinstates peace. When Jon Osterman disintegrates following an experiment gone amiss, he still appears to be more or less the same person, only now he can perceive the future, present and past simultaneously. Dr Manhattan has gained the ability to alter physical matter with a mere thought. But continually becoming increasingly disengaged from what is essential to humans, he finds it more and more impossible to relate to humanity. His very supremacy alienates him. The estrangement, however, differs from that suffered by, for instance, the Hulk. It is not coincidental that Moore's superhero is a scientist in the mould of the 1960s superheroes, but whereas Dr Banner and Dr Manhattan both recognize that they are isolated from their environment by their powers, Dr Manhattan does not articulate any sort of anxiety about this development. In keeping with the aloof and ethereal being he has become and in contrast to the 1960s superheroes who derived their powers from accidents involving radioactivity, he does not bemoan the loss of a bond to humanity.

When the Wind Blows is a graphic novel by children's author Raymond Briggs published in 1982 and translated into an animated movie in 1986 by Jimmy Murakami. It is possibly one of the gloomiest narratives about devastated lives ever told. A covert, heterodiegetic narrator traces the lives of James and Hilda Bloggs, an elderly British moon-faced couple in the days immediately before and after nuclear holocaust. We witness James's preparatory attempt to build a makeshift fallout shelter, Hilda doing household chores and their conversations together, presented in a rather rigid grid that consists of small panels that are arranged in sequence. This scheme is only interrupted when double pages depicting the imminent threat or memory passages are inserted. It is therefore all the more significant that the grid is first absent entirely on the double page immediately following the dropping of the bomb and is then slowly reintroduced as a variation of the network of panels on the next double page. Just as Scarry claims that the depiction of the weapon or the wound has to suffice because pain destroys language, large-scale destruction caused by a nuclear holocaust itself cannot be shown. Instead, Briggs represents the traumatic event by the dissolution of the narrated world that is mirrored in the suspension of the narrative technique, i.e. the panel grid.

What makes this particular narrative so depressing is the stark juxtaposition of the peaceful, pastoral setting, the couple's unwavering trust in science and their government, and the dire consequences of the radioactivity released. The Bloggs' blindly patriotic faith and their stoic belief that they will be rescued even as the reader comprehends that this will not happen, results in a gentle yet dark humor. This again is coupled with a drawing style and layout that is heavily suggestive of traditional children's books, which renders the major contradictions and ambiguities of *When the Wind Blows* even more powerful: on the one hand, the Bloggs seem to possess a notion of the immense devastative power of radioactivity, on the other hand, even when they themselves are exposed to the aftermath of the bomb, they do not associate the severe impact on the environment, their house and their bodies with the effects of radiation but with various unlikely scenarios. The couple takes the government warnings extremely seriously and builds an insubstantial fallout shelter according to government regulations, but Hilda in particular seems entirely preoccupied with keeping her cushions clean (8, panels 1-3) and avoiding stains on clothes: "You can wear your old clothes for The Bomb and save your best for afterwards" (17, panels 4-5). They are afraid of a prospective war, hence the adherence to the government's somewhat ludicrous instructions on the fallout shelter, and yet they harbor nostalgic feelings for the last war they witnessed: "Yes, it was nice in The War, really … The Shelters …. the Blackout …. the All Clear" (7, panel 3).

But the juxtaposition of adverse elements goes beyond the character level: several double pages, inserted into the otherwise small-paneled narrative, depict the looming threat on land (4-5), in the air (10-11) and under the sea (14-15). The multihued and bright color scheme of the paneled pages is starkly contrasted with the dark and sinister scenes depicted on these double pages. In addition, the double pages each contain a caption box saying "meanwhile, on a distant plain" (4), "meanwhile, in the distant sky" (10) and "meanwhile, in a distant ocean" respectively. The word 'meanwhile' has a long tradition in comics where it is frequently employed to achieve suspense through simultaneous storytelling:[10] The reader is alerted to the fact that something else is taking place concurrently, i.e. the enemy is approaching on several levels while the unsuspecting couple has tea. 'Distant', by contrast, suggests that the danger is nowhere close. In direct contact, the two words make strange bedfellows, with a meaning that the reader might find difficult to gauge.

From the quasi-otherworldliness of Dr Manhattan, as sketched in *Watchmen*, to the easily identifiable, down-to-earth couple as delineated by Briggs, each of the characters considered in this section represents at least one feature of the consequences of radioactivity. Even though Dr Manhattan does not struggle with his powers, he is alienated from humanity by the effects of the accident. The Bloggs, by contrast, represent the other end of the scale, namely slow death as a result of the bomb. By means of differing approaches to character depiction, layout and color, the authors and artists here discussed have found varying methods of addressing the topic of radioactive lives in comic books and graphic novels.

4. Biographies and Scientific Discoveries: Lauren Redniss's *Tale of Love and Fallout*

Lauren Redniss is an award-winning US-American writer, cartoonist and artist[11] who in late 2010 published *Radioactive: Marie and Pierre Curie. A Tale of Love and Fallout,* which was nominated by *The New York Times* for the Pulitzer Prize. In the year of its publication, it was also a finalist for the *LA Times* Book Prize in the science and technology category and the first visual book to be named a finalist for the National Book Award in Non-Fiction. *Radioactive* is a stunning biographical graphic novel-cum-history lesson-cum-love story which recounts the lives of two brilliant and devoted scientists and their contributions to science and medicine. Redniss explains the concepts of radioactivity, half-life and nuclear fission and explores the implications, both positive and negative, of Marie Curie's ground-breaking discovery of radium.

Radioactive has been called an "illustrated biography" (Garner) and a *bande dessinée* or a graphic novel (Nye, Harayda). What is obvious is that Redniss chose to

[10] It has even acquired a questionable notoriety: Today, it is often used to create humor rather than tension.

[11] Redniss was a fellow at the Cullman Center for Scholars & Writers at the New York Public Library in 2008-2009 and became a New York Institute for the Humanities Fellow in 2010. In 2012 she was the recipient of a Guggenheim Fellowship and was Artist-in-Residence at the American Museum of Natural History. She teaches at Parsons The New School for Design in New York City.

combine text and pictures in order to explore a new way of re/presenting radioactivity and nuclear disaster. Since the text-picture relationships are rich and highly complex – there is, for example a technopaignium (i.e. shaped poem) in prose (124-125) – and the stunning pictures are more than mere illustrations, 'graphic novel' seems to be the most adequate genre term for *Radioactive*, even if Redniss "modifies the format of graphic novels as she [...] omits the usual strips or panels and encloses her text in more creative ways on black-and-white, two-toned, or multi-colored spreads" (Harayda). Images are the hub of *Radioactive* and appear on almost every page or serve as background for the text, which is set in a typeface specially created by Redniss.[12] By mixing a love story with the scientific history of radioactivity Redniss has created a unique work difficult to categorize. It documents its "tale of love and fallout" with archival and published sources, including Eve Curie's biography of her mother, *Madame Curie* (originally published in 1937) and Susan Quinn's 1995 *Marie Curie: A Life*, and blends historical photographs, facsimiles of original documents and maps with Redniss's own text and images, i.e. drawings as well as rich and colorful illustrations of elements, people and places, which collectively render the story of Marie and Pierre Curie.

Radioactive is a work of art which combines its impressive artful visual material with equally great prose writing that has been characterized as "long, literate and supple" (Garner). At first glance *Radioactive* might appear to be a children's book, when in fact it addresses adult readers whose curiosity and anticipation are attracted before it is even opened: compared to other biographies and graphic novels, it is oversized; the cover (fig. 1) with its maize yellow, orange and different shades of green is very alluring, as is the title and playful subtitle (radioactivity, love and fallout). The pose of Marie Curie's turned away head on the cover, which Alan Lockwood has compared with Andrew Wyeth's fraught landscape, "Christina's World", and Gerhard Richter's portrait of his daughter Betty, adds an element of suspense, thrill and mystery, as does the back cover with its different colors ranging from royal to pale blue and white and its eye-catching words "Sabotage! Temptation! Duels! Revelation!". There is also an unexpected and enchantingly haptic element to the book. The green part at the top of the cover and the outlines of Marie Curie's bust silhouette are of a tactile velvety material, as are the spine and parts of the back cover illustrations. On a bedside table, the book will again surprise its reader when it 'radiates' in the dark since its cover is printed with glow-in-the-dark ink. It is clear that this book is not only meant to be read but also experienced in its physical materiality. As readers we relish each picture and its accompanying text which often runs across and over the pages, hence constantly blurring the boundaries between word and image. Some of the pictures are also highly scary and unsettling.

[12] The book ends with "A Note on CYANOTYPE Printing" that explains the process used by Redniss to create the illuminative images of her alluring book: she made negatives from her drawings, using those to create the image. Aesthetically, she felt that the white boundary line captures what "Marie Curie describes as radium's 'spontaneous luminosity'", its internal glow (199).

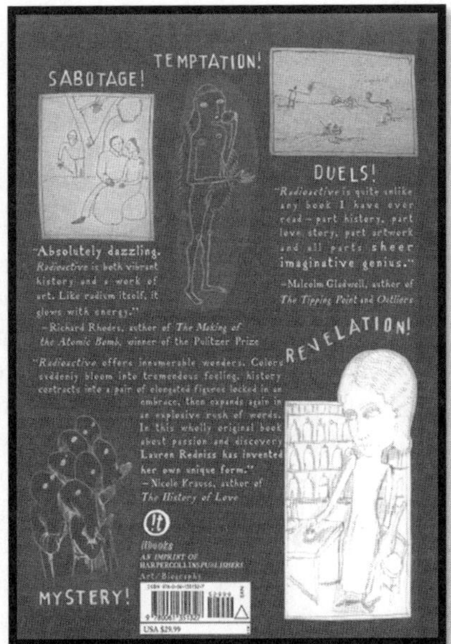

Fig.1: Lauren Redniss, cover of Radioactive

A brief synopsis of the story runs as follows:[13] In 1891, the 24-year old Marya alias Marie Sklodowska moves from Warsaw to Paris, obtains a degree in both mathematics and physics from the Faculté des Sciences at the Sorbonne as "one of just 23 women in a student body of some 1800" (25) and eventually meets Pierre Curie, a fellow-scientist. Redniss draws them with elongated Modigliani faces (Garner), hatched eyelid rims and pale outlines which seem to hint from the start at the dangers of radioactivity. Pierre studies crystalline structures and offers to share his laboratory space with Marie. They fall in love, get married and spend their honeymoon in 1895 on a bicycle tour, "riding along the coast of Brittany and into the French countryside" (34). The warm earthen colors of brown, yellow and dark orange used by Redniss not only symbolize the feelings of the couple, but they are repeated just a few pages later in a photograph of a nuclear explosion. The author's intricate use of color patterns as displayed in the first few pages makes the reader immediately aware of the ambiguous qualities of radioactivity: the "spontaneous luminosity" (51) of the two compounds of radium (chloride and bromide, 54-55), which discharges a faint-blue light, is represented by Redniss's use of blues,

[13] Redniss presents *Radioactive* in two parts: part I, consisting of chapters 1-3, is mainly biographical; the titles of the chapters refer to characteristics of the material the Curies worked with, the discovery of radioactivity as well as the mutual emotional attraction of Marie and Pierre. Part II (chapters 4-9) illuminates the Curies' revelations around radium, their rise in scientific circles, the effect radiation had on their own health, and the consequences of their discovery for the world.

and the radiance and heat emitted by radioactive elements are alluded to by the bright orange and red colors in other images.[14] This color scheme is present throughout the book.

Discoveries and developments at the turn of the twentieth century resonate in Redniss's graphic novel, and these include not only technical discoveries, but also the prevailing belief in immateriality, invisibility, spiritualism and the power to communicate with the dead. Redniss's comments on the history of science and the blurred boundary between science and magic are highly illuminating: "If invisible light could pass through flesh and expose the human skeleton, was it so fantastical to believe in levitation, in telekinesis, in communication with the dead?" (52) Clearly, the Curies' discovery of two new elements, radium and polonium, heralded a new scientific age. For instance, at the time when the Curies are celebrating the birth of their daughter Irène, in Germany the physicist Wilhelm Röntgen discovers an invisible light which he calls X-rays. Röntgen's wife "intuited the power of her husband's discovery – to intercept, as well as to hasten, death" (Redniss 42). While new discoveries such as X-rays, radium and radioactivity fascinated people at the turn of the twentieth century and this "series of invisible forces were radically transforming daily life" (52), Redniss shows that from the start the scientists who discovered X-rays and radioactivity were aware of the ambivalence of their discoveries, i.e. medical advantages for surgery and cancer, but also of the potentially dangerous effects and the possibilities of misuse.

The tension between life and death is indeed conspicuously present in the rest of the book, for instance in the passage about World War I during which Marie Curie developed X-ray field labs:

> Marie began assembling hospital X-ray units. Then she brought the technology directly to the battlefield, rigging an automobile with tubes and screens and electricity to create a mobile X-ray facility. By the war's end, Marie and Irène had outfitted 18 such vehicles, which came to be known as 'petites Curies', along with 2000 stationary units. Some of the cars saw as many as 100,000 soldiers receive treatment. No longer were doctors performing blind exploratory surgeries on already damaged bodies. [...] The work exposed both women to large amounts of radiation. (156, 159)

The precariousness of human life exposed to radioactivity is showcased in Marie Curie's medical records held at the Curie Archives, on which the following passage is based:

[14] All reviewers of *Radioactivity* underline the beauty of Redniss's eerie and ethereal drawings, her rich pictures and her color pattern which are coupled with an equally beautiful typeface: "The book is illustrated in blues, oranges and reds, as well as in a lighter blue that is meant to suggest what Marie Curie referred to as the 'spontaneous luminosity' of radium, which emits a faint-blue light. [...] The bright orange and red colors in other images remind readers of the energy, the glow and the heat of radioactive substances; in one of the book's embedded vignettes, these colors are explicitly recalled by a survivor of the atomic bomb dropped on Hiroshima: 'Suddenly all the windows in front of me became red. It was a beautiful color, like the sunrise mingled with orange.'" (Nye)

> Years of radiation exposure had ravaged Marie's health. Her fingers were barnacled with fibrous lesions from handling radium. She chronicled her own deterioration as laboratory data in neat columns on graph paper. Body temperature, color and amount of urine discharged, 'crises and pus', were logged at multiple intervals throughout each day. In the margins, she tracked the pain in her body. [...] At dawn on July 4, 1934, Marie Curie passed away. The cause of death was 'aplastic pernicious anemia' due to prolonged radiation exposure. She was sixty-six years old. (168, 171)

This is one of several sections which cover the effects of long-term radium exposure, from which Marie and Pierre Curie both suffered. In addition, in chapter 6 (titled "Half-Life") Redniss presents the story of young women who worked with radium for the US Radium Corporation in New Jersey in the 1920s and experienced "long series of crippling symptoms – decomposing jaws, bleeding gums, severe anemia, immobilizing weakness" (90). Radium, we are told by Redniss, is a "'bone-seeker'. Introduced into the body, it replaces the calcium in bones, causing them to deteriorate" (90).

Initially, Redniss was struck by the fact that today's weaponry, medicine, energy and their implications, all link back to the Curies' romance in nineteenth-century Paris, and her graphic novel mentions some more recent consequences of the Curies' discovery of radium, such as the cranial radiation treatments that enabled a 14-year-old Rhode Island boy named Daniel Fass to survive his non-Hodgkins lymphoma (a massive tumor next to his heart and lungs, 70-71). But again, Redniss also presents the precarious disadvantages of radioactivity, which range from the partial meltdown of two nuclear reactors at Three Mile Island near Harrisburg in 1979 (102-103) that produced mutant plant specimens, to the disaster of Chernobyl in 1986 (114-115). There are several one- or two-page peripheral stories, such as one on Irving S. Lowen (77-79), a theoretical physicist who worked on the Manhattan project and became paranoid about Germany's progress in the nuclear arms war, as is documented in his declassified FBI file (78-79); or the mini-narratives on atomic tests in the Pacific Ocean and Nevada during the Cold War period (138-139, 140-141). These interspersed "vignettes" (Nye) are subplots, and although it is obvious that there can be no clickable text function, Karen Sandstrom has rightly pointed out the similarities between Redniss's *Radioactive* and hypertextually encoded fiction.

This documentary graphic novel is predominantly presented via the voice of its omniscient author, Lauren Redniss, who presides over the collage-like presentation of the lives of the Curies as well as the history of their monumental scientific discovery like a museum curator. But there are also passages in the text which are taken from diaries and memoirs and are thus told directly by people affected by exposure to radioactivity, such as the passages relating to the Curies mentioned above. Another example is Sadae Kasaoke's description of her father's body after he had been severely injured by the first atomic bomb detonated above Hiroshima:

> Fallen roof tiles and plaster of houses were scattered everywhere. About 9 A.M., a man in the neighborhood, who had been downtown, returned. He was so badly burned, his skin peeled so that his face and arms looked pink. He shouted, 'With a flash everything was destroyed'. That night, we heard that Father had taken shelter in a relative's house in Okocho. My brother went there and came back with him in a two-wheeled cart. My father,

> lying on a door board, looked dead. His face was swollen and his clothes were burned off, leaving him naked. I could identify him just by his voice. We had no medicine, so we grated cucumbers and potatoes to make a dressing. His body was burned not only on the surface but also inside. (83)

As shown in earlier examples, and in spite of *Radioactive*'s strikingly beautiful visual art, the two aspects of radioactivity, its power to both save and to utterly destroy life, remain always present. It is all the more topical that only a few months after the publication of Redniss's graphic novel nuclear disaster occurred at the atomic power plant in Fukushima in March 2011.

Comic books and graphic novels reflect and negotiate that part of Western and particularly American cultural history that is intimately related to the discovery of radioactivity and its precarious negative sides. As our examples demonstrate, radioactivity has released a range of polarized hopes and anxieties. As claimed in thesis 8, the mass-marketed genres discussed here offer special aesthetic and ethical experiences, they have social implications and should hence be considered a means of political participation. Since regional and global risk scenarios which involve nuclear disaster challenge both conventional language and commonsense reasoning, its representation, too, is precarious – a precariousness which the medium of the comic book or graphic novel can cope with ingeniously. A future collaboration of comics researchers, literary scholars, psychologists and picture specialists will have to investigate further in what way text-picture combinations lend themselves to present the unrepresentable and whether the pictures, visual symbolism and color codes used in intermedial storytelling have indeed the potential to extend their readers' emotional, affective and ethical participation in face of precarious lives.

Works Cited

Primary Sources

Briggs, Raymond. *When the Wind Blows*. London: Penguin Books, 1982.

Eisner, Will (w/a). *A Contract with God and Other Tenement Stories: A Graphic Novel*. 1979. New York: W. W. Norton and Company, 2006.

Gaiman, Neil (w) and various (a). *The Absolute Sandman*. 1989-1996. 5 vols. New York: DC Comics, 2006-2011.

Moore, Alan (w) and Dave Gibbons (a). *Watchmen*. 12 vols. 1986-1987. Trade Paperback Edition. New York: DC Comics, 2005.

Moore, Alan (w) and David Lloyd (a). *V for Vendetta*. 10 vols. 1982-1989. Trade Paperback Edition. New York: DC Comics, 2005.

Redniss, Lauren. *Radioactive: Pierre and Marie Curie. A Tale of Love and Fallout*. New York: Harper Collins, 2010.

Satrapi, Marjane. *Persepolis*. 2000. London: Vintage, 2008.

Shute, Nevil. *On the Beach*. 1957. London: Vintage Classics, 2009.

Spiegelman, Art (w/a). *Maus*. 1986-1992. Trade Paperback Edition. New York: Pantheon Books, 2003.

Secondary Sources

Beck, Ulrich. *Risikogesellschaft: Auf dem Weg in eine andere Moderne*. Frankfurt: Suhrkamp, 1986.

Berger, James. *After the End: Representations of Post-Apocalypse*. Minneapolis: University of Minnesota Press, 1999.

Boyer, Paul S. et al. *The Enduring Vision: A History of the American People*. 5th ed. Boston, MA: Houghton Mifflin Company, 2005.

Cowsill, Alan et al. *DC Comics Year by Year: A Visual Chronicle*. London: DK Publishing, 2010.

Garner, Dwight. "The Curies, Seen Through an Artist's Eyes." *The New York Times*: *Books*. 21 Dec. 2010. Retrieved 12 June 2013. <http://www.nytimes.com/2010/12/22/books/22book.html?_r=0>.

Gibbons, Dave, Chip Kidd, and Mike Essl. *Watching the Watchmen*. London: Titan Books, 2008.

Harayda, Janice. "Marie and Pierre Curie, Exposed – Lauren Redniss's *Radioactive*." *One-Minute Book Reviews*. 26 Nov. 2011. Retrieved 14 June 2013. <http://oneminutebookreviews.wordpress.com/2011/11/26/marie-and-pierre-curie-exposed-lauren-rednisss-radioactive/>.

Heise, Ursula K. "Afterglow: Chernobyl and the Everyday." *Nature in Literary and Cultural Studies: Transatlantic Conversations on Ecocriticism*. Ed. Catrin Gersdorf and Sylvia Mayer. Amsterdam: Rodopi, 2006. 177-207.

Hoppeler, Stephanie. "Continuity in Comic Books and Comic Book Continuity: Serialized North-American Comic Books of the 1989s." Diss. (Typescript). University of Bern, 2013.

Hoppeler, Stephanie, and Gabriele Rippl. "Continuity, Fandom und Serialität in anglo-amerikanischen Comic Books." *Populäre Serialität: Narration – Evolution – Distinktion. Zum seriellen Erzählen seit dem 19. Jahrhundert*. Ed. Frank Kelleter. Bielefeld: Transcript, 2012. 367-379.

Kappas, Arvid, and Marion G. Müller. "Bild und Emotion – ein neues Forschungsfeld." *Publizistik* 51.1 (March 2006): 3-23.

Keen, Suzanne. *Empathy and the Novel*. Oxford: Oxford University Press, 2010.

—. "Fast Tracks to Narrative Empathy: Anthropomorphism and Dehumanization in Graphic Narratives." *SubStance* 124, 40.1 (2011): 135-155.

Levitz, Paul. *75 Years of DC Comics: The Art of Modern Myth-Making*. Köln: Taschen, 2010.

Lockwood, Alan. "LOVE + RADIANCE: Marie Curie in Redniss's *Radioactive*." *The Brooklyn Rail*. 4 Mar. 2011. Retrieved 3 Aug. 2013. <http://www.brooklynrail.org/2011/03/express/love-radiance-marie-curie-in-lauren-rednisss-radioactive>.

McCloud, Scott. *Understanding Comics: The Invisible Art*. New York: Harper Perennial, 1993.

Nöth, Winfried. *Handbuch der Semiotik*. 2nd ed. Stuttgart and Weimar: Metzler, 2000.

Nye, Mary Jo. "Of Passion and Polonium." *American Scientist* May-June 2011. Retrieved 14 June 2013. <http://www.americanscientist.org/bookshelf/pub/of-passion-and-polonium>.

Petersen, Robert S. *Comics, Manga and Graphic Novels: A History of Graphic Narrative*. Santa Barbara: Praeger, 2011.

Pratt, Henry John. "Medium Specificity and the Ethics of Comics." *Storyworlds* 1 (2009): 97-113.

Rifas, Leonard. "Cartooning and Nuclear Power: From Industry Advertising to Activist Uprising and Beyond." *PS: Political Science and Politics* 40 (April 2007): 255-260.

—. "Cold War Comics." *International Journal of Comic Art* 2 (Spring 2001): 3-32.

Rippl, Gabriele, and Lukas Etter. "Intermediality, Transmediality and Graphic Narrative." *From Comic Strips to Graphic Novels*. Ed. Daniel Stein and Jan-Noël Thon. Berlin: De Gruyter, 2013. 191-218.

Sabin, Roger. *Comics, Comix and Graphic Novels: A History of Graphic Art*. London: Phaidon, 2008.

Sandstrom, Karen. "Lauren Redniss' *Radioactive* Gives Us Love in the Time of Radium." 27 Dec. 2010. Retrieved 3 Aug. 2013. <http://www.cleveland.com/books/index.ssf/2010/12/lauren_redniss_radioactive_giv.html>.

Scarry, Elaine. *The Body in Pain: The Making and Unmaking of the World*. New York: Oxford University Press, 1985.

Szasz, Ferenc Morton. *Atomic Comics: Cartoonists Confront the Nuclear World*. Reno: University of Nevada Press, 2012.

Taylor, Charles. *Modern Social Imaginaries*. Durham, NC: Duke University Press, 2004.

Withrow, Steven, and Alexander Danner. *Character Design for Graphic Novels*. Mies: Roto Vision, 2007.

Zapf, Hubert. "Literary Ecology and the Ethics of Texts." *NLH* 39 (2009): 847-868.

—. "The State of Ecocriticism and the Function of Literature as Cultural Ecology." *Nature in Literary and Cultural Studies: Transatlantic Conversations on Ecocriticism*. Ed. Catrin Gersdorf and Sylvia Mayer. Amsterdam: Rodopi, 2006. 49-69.

Ellen Dengel-Janic

The Precariousness of Postcolonial Geographies: Amitav Ghosh's *The Shadow Lines* and *The Hungry Tide*

1. Introduction

Amitav Ghosh's novels to date are considered creative re-workings of Indian history. His narratives do not simply follow the chronology of colonial and postcolonial India, but they are carefully enriched with spatial metaphors, specific regional settings and characteristic landscapes. One might ask whether Ghosh prefers to tell stories that engage with the idea of the nation from a postcolonial perspective or whether he focuses more closely on specific local histories such as, for example, the history of Bengal. Ghosh's penchant for what one critic has called "cartographic narratives" (Mallot 261) is noticeable in his more recent novels, too. These cartographic narratives move across various times and spaces such as, for example, the urban Bengal and Bangladesh in *The Shadow Lines* (1988) and the rural Bay of Bengal in *The Hungry Tide* (2005).

In his work, Ghosh critiques various forms of social precariousness produced by history and the modern nation state as well as the forces of nature and a threatening geographical space. *The Hungry Tide,* for example, showcases the precarious social position of characters as undivided from their perilous and shifting locations in nature. If precariousness is not just connected to social and political life, but also to geography and nature, one might extend in this respect Judith Butler's suggestion that we need to re-think what it means to be human from the standpoint of an ontological precariousness: "There are ways of distributing vulnerability, differential forms of allocation that make some populations more subject to arbitrary violence than others" (xii). Butler uses Levinas to explain the connection between precariousness, power and discourse:

> But let us remember that Levinas has told us that the face – which is the face of the Other, and so the ethical demand made by the Other – is the vocalisation of agony that is not yet language or no longer language, the one by which we are wakened to the precariousness of the Other's life, the one that rouses at once the temptation to murder and the interdiction against it. (139)

Ghosh's postcolonial take on Indian history is grounded in the belief that the Other, both the colonial subject as well as the subaltern classes in post-Independence India, need to be rendered visible and redeemed from their continuing marginalisation. The groups that are marginalised and thus seen as the Other, the refugees, threatened communities as well as lower-class and lower-caste men and women are especially "subject to arbitrary violence" (Butler xii). Ghosh portrays the experience of violence in *The*

Shadow Lines as well as in *The Hungry Tide*. While the characters are caught in recurrent and multiple displacements, Ghosh outlines the socio-spatial dimension of postcolonial precariousness. Opening up the discussion of Otherness and subalternity to the question of its spatial and geographical significance, he narrates spatially determined stories of characters in extremely precarious historical moments and under existential threat. In this chapter, Ghosh's portrayals of two different kinds of spatial precariousness will be discussed in detail: firstly, in *The Shadow Lines*, the author uses the image of the map to show the forces of exclusion and danger coming from borders; secondly, in *The Hungry Tide*, he depicts the geographical and political perilousness in the region of the Sunderbans. One might regard Ghosh's insistent foregrounding of different types of cartographic narratives as a broadening of the scope of postcolonial writing that often revolves around history and historical narrative. He employs the representation of place in order to criticise hierarchies and mechanisms of control that bear on the social and natural world. Furthermore, his spatially organised narratives will be discussed as relevant comments on the social and political forms of precariousness that are depicted in almost all of his novels.

2. The Significance of Precarious Geographies

As commonly known, the term 'precarious' is frequently employed in reference to labour. Some critics have observed that it is the "practice of labour mobility" which results in precarious forms of labour:

> Importantly, capital has always tried to shore up its own precariousness through the control of labour and, in particular, the mobility of labour [...]. Because the depreciation and precarisation of migrant labour threatens to engulf the workforce as a whole (and because the subjective mobility and resistance of migrants tests the limits of capitalist control), their position becomes the social anticipation of a political option to struggle against the general development of labour and life in the contemporary world. (Neilson and Rossiter)

Not only is precarious labour central to the history of capitalism, but the figure of the undocumented migrant can be considered emblematic of the workings of the capitalist market and its treatment of human labour. At the same time, what Neilson and Rossiter make clear is that the migrant's mobility "test[s] the limits of capitalist control".

If the migrant's mobility is both the condition of precariousness and the possibility to contest capitalism, the uncertain geographical locations of Ghosh's protagonists need to be examined more closely. In order to grasp the nature of the representations of precarious geographies it is essential that one uncovers the underlying concepts of space in broader terms. Critics have argued that Ghosh has ingeniously shown that one's idea of a geographical or political region is not defined by objective coordinates and systematic maps but by personal and subjective perceptions (cf. for example Mallot). Edward Soja's concept of spatiality helps to unravel the different spatial dimensions that affect our understanding of space:

> The presentation of concrete spatiality is always wrapped in the complex and diverse representations of human perception and cognition, without any necessity of direct and determined correspondence between the two. These representations, as semiotic imagery and cognitive mappings, as ideas and ideologies, play a powerful role in shaping the spatiality of social life. There can be no challenge to the existence of this humanized, mental space, a spatialized mentalite. (121)

Human perception and cognition as much as social organisation of space determine how we perceive and experience particular places. Thus, one needs to take into account that maps and cartographic representations of space demand to be expanded and complemented with means of perception and cognition, social constructions and ideologies. Ghosh's literary rendering of spatial conditions proves insightful given the multidimensionality of the literary work: including setting, narrative voice and perception of place, atmospheric and symbolic use of space, characters' understanding of places as well as the greater scope of ideological and cultural notions of space and place. If we consider Ghosh's works as spatial narratives, their contribution to conceptual understandings of space consists of the interplay of all the various spatial aspects mentioned above. As Azaryahu and Foote have recently argued, "often spatial narratives involve a complex configuration of geographic elements including buildings, markers, memorials, and inscriptions positioned with great care to provide a spatial story-line or to capture the key locational and chronological relations of an historical event" (3). Geographic elements such as the homes and houses, countries and borders, as well as cities and landscapes in Ghosh's novels are imagined through the stories and memories of the characters and, subsequently, the narrator assembles a larger chronology of the historical storyline tied to particular spaces. Thus Soja's spatiality (physical, mental and social) is completed by a historical chronology deepening our understanding of space.

The relationship between space and precariousness is centrally discussed in Ghosh's *The Shadow Lines*, where changing political situations shape the borders of nation states and thus place some parts of the population into contested border regions. The title refers to the nature of dividing lines that are difficult to see yet are present and cast a shadow on the nation's history. Crossing and transgressing these "shadow lines", the historically evolved and still shifting borders of nations and cultures, also become central issues for the novel's characters: for some this act of border crossing signifies a widening of their horizons, yet for others it ends in a loss of identity, and, for the protagonist, even in the loss of his life. *The Hungry Tide* also depicts characters in precarious geo-political contexts, with the additional impact of the natural environment on human existence. Thus, Ghosh broadens his scope by including nature in his representation of human precariousness. His preoccupation in this novel is still with Indian history and the formation of the nation state, yet, by focussing on one particular region, the Sunderbans, he also explores the difficulties faced by the inhabitants: those who simply want to survive in a hostile natural environment and those whose interest lies in the uniqueness of the ecosystem.

3. *The Shadow Lines*: Maps versus Lived Experience

In *The Shadow Lines*, what is most at stake are the lives of those people who have affiliations on both sides of the line of division and have become victims of family histories that were divided by national boundaries. The story revolves around an extended Indian family, the Datta Chaudharis from Calcutta, spanning the time from the Second World War to the 1980s: told by an unnamed narrator, the lives of the grandmother Tha'mma, a school headmistress and former nationalist activist, her nephew Tridib and her granddaughter Ila gradually unfold. At the centre of the story lies Tridib's tragic death in the almost forgotten riots that took place in Dhaka (1963-64), Bangladesh's capital, and are presented as parallel events that uncannily connect the history of India to that of its neighbouring country.

But the story also covers the Datta Chaudharis' many travels and visits to London where they form a friendship with an English family, the Prices, that lasts several generations. How Ghosh intertwines the characters' spatial movement and their perceptions of history is shown in the following scene. The narrator undertakes a journey to London where his cousin Ila and her friend Nick show him around. When they visit Brick Lane, Ila and Nick, who might be expected to be more familiar with the place than the narrator as they lived there for many years, are in fact less knowledgeable about their surroundings. The reader is presented with the narrator's recollection of his uncle's Tridib's visit to London with his family during World War II:

> This was the window of Dan's bedroom, I decided. It was easy to see how the windowpanes might have been blacked out with ink-blackened newspapers. It was the window that Dan had opened that September night in 1940, when he'd grown tired of trying to sleep on the mattress below the stairs, with the others. (102)

This is an invented depiction of the death of Dan, a young Englishman, whose tragic death in that September night in 1940 must have been told as a wartime story to Tridib and then, much later, to the narrator as one of the many stories that Tridib tells about his travels. The London house in the 1960s that the narrator observes on the level of the contemporary narrative is thus layered with the stories about the war that he had heard from others. His perception of the actual inner city of London is moulded by the historical narrative of this place. The narrator's historical knowledge and the contemporary physical reality of the house thus blend into one spatial-temporal impression that is related to the reader.

There are numerous instances in the novel that show the interconnectedness of time and place in the perception of the characters. But also the very fundamental structure of the novel is based on spatial conditions: its two-part structure, with the first part entitled "Going Away" and the second "Coming Home", suggests that Ghosh's concern circles around the main themes of home and exile, of belonging and alienation. All characters oscillate between those two poles and provide a spectrum of journeys, routes of discovery, making and leaving homes.[1] If one regards the characters' locations as essential

[1] Shameem Black argues that homes and houses figure quite dominantly in Ghosh's work: "the idea of home emerges most forcefully as a double form of physical and social architecture.

to the novel's plot and theme, the centrality of space and geography is unquestionable. On the one hand, Ghosh's range of spaces and places covers India, Bangladesh and England, on the other hand, he also adds personal imagination to the characters' depictions and recollections of these places. Firstly, the anonymous narrator assembles the memories and stories of other characters to chart a diverse cartography of their travels. Secondly, it is shown that imagination always affects the characters' journeys:

> I could not persuade her that a place does not merely exist, that it has to be invented in one's imagination; that her practical bustling London was no less invented than mine, neither more nor less true, only very far apart. It was not her fault that she could not understand, for as Tridib often said of her, the inventions she lived in moved with her, so that although she had lived in many places, she had never travelled at all. (21)

In this case, Tridib's understanding of space is that it is a conceived notion, similar to what Lefebvre calls "perceived space", i.e. space that evokes, and is evoked by its inhabitants, that is produced by images and symbols, by descriptions and signs (38-40). Ila seems to illustrate a particular case of spatial perception as she imagines one space that is always present. Never having experienced home due to the fact that Ila's parents travelled as diplomats across the globe, she relies on places such as airports that always look similar and thus provide a certain sense of familiarity. In contrast, the narrator, through the mediation and storytelling of Tridib, imagines places he has never visited and 'perceives' them with the help of his already pre-existing imagination as he succinctly declares that "Tridib has given me worlds to travel in and eyes to see them with" (21). Thus, perceived space is undoubtedly regarded as more significant than geographical space.

At a crucial point in the novel, imagined and subjectively perceived space collides forcefully with the geo-political reality, for instance when the narrator's grandmother expects the newly created border between East Pakistan and India to be visible from the plane flying over it when they travel to their ancestral home in Dhaka:

> [O]ne evening when we were sitting out in the garden she wanted to know whether she would be able to see the border between India and East Pakistan from the plane. When my father laughed and said, why, did she really think the border was a long black line with green on one side and scarlet on the other, like it was some school atlas, she was not so much offended as puzzled. (151)

The grandmother, an educated woman who participated in the *swadeshi* movement, is of course not so naïve as to believe that the actual landscape is shaped like a map but she still expects the Partition to leave visible traces, to reflect the struggle, violence and

Houses, flats, roofs and domestic artefacts shape the inner world of the novel, while the bonds of extended kinship networks provide metaphorical structures within which the characters develop over time. While houses and families are not synonyms for each other, they both gesture towards domestic structures of feeling that seek to place individuals within literal and figurative forms of dwelling. Through these physical and symbolic spaces, Ghosh explores one vision of what Kwame Anthony Appiah calls 'rooted cosmopolitanism'" (46).

suffering that accompanied it. This scene makes it obvious that Ghosh is indeed concerned with maps and locations that have been under great historical pressure in instances when people are confronted with the arbitrary yet exclusionist nature of borders. Mallot suggests that the problem with maps can be laid out as follows:

> [M]aps generally tell single stories, alternative versions of a past are either ignored or erased; to draw a map anew – in the case of the quickly determined, hastily arranged Partition of 1947 – is to visually wipe away a particular 'past'. More broadly, [South Asian] authors claim, new national maps have stood at odds with individual memories, with drastic consequences for individuals struggling to reconcile lived experience with narratives. (261)

While the national map that enacts the Partition of India in 1947 affects the lives of the characters in *The Shadow Lines*, and this is what the grandmother expects to see with her own eyes, Ghosh's narrative assembles different perceptions of the past that co-exist in contradicting ways with the greater narrative of the nation and its rigidly enforced borders.

According to the grandmother, the two newly formed nation states should make their borderline visible and thus make it possible to distinguish them, and show that the state has control over territory and the identities that are assigned and distributed accordingly. In other words, space itself should confirm the historical change and political organisation of the nation(s). This historical manifestation of national borders is in fact quite similar to the politics of imperialism. Paul Carter has aptly shown how spatial conquest and naming has contributed to the imposition and expansion of colonial rule. In his postcolonial critique of Australia's history, Carter claims that *space*, in a colonial context, becomes the *stage* for imperialist history. In this context, naming and mapping turn into tools in the imperialist conquest of 'new' territories.[2] It is especially the act of naming during the period of colonialism, and its importance for his analysis of its spatial history, that Carter draws attention to:

> This metaphorical way of speaking is a pointer to the way spatial history must interpret its sources. It also indicates, concisely and poetically, the *cultural* place where spatial history begins: not in a particular year, nor in a particular place, but *in the act of naming*. For by the act of place-naming, space is transformed symbolically into a place, that is, a space with a history. And, by the same token, the namer inscribes his passage permanently on the world, making a metaphorical word-place which others may one day inhabit and by which, in the meantime, he asserts his own place in history. (xxiv)

[2] It is also noteworthy that Carter suggests in his work *The Road to Botany Bay* that: "It points to a kind of history where travelling is a process of *continually* beginning, continually ending, where discovery and settlement belong to the same exploratory process. The 'facts' of this spatial history are not houses and clearings, but phenomena as they appear to the traveller, as his intentional gaze conjures them up. They are the directions and distances in which houses and clearings *may* be found and founded" (xxiv).

It is through the act of naming that a place can be owned, administrated and governed by the colonial authority. Thus the process of naming and mapping becomes always vitally important in cases of ambiguity and struggle over land and territory, in instances where territorial property and power are in fact contested. The border area or zone is such a prime example of contested territory. Kearney's analysis of the US-Mexican border disputes can be taken as paradigmatic of geo-political border struggles in general:

> In recent years the Border Area, after a claimed 'century of quiescence' since the Mexican American War of 1848, again becomes contested terrain. Now, however, it is not territory *per se* that is being contested, but instead personal identities and movements of persons, and cultural and political hegemony of peoples. A Latino reconquest of much of the northern side has already taken place. But this Latino cultural and demographic ascendency is not congruent with jural territorial realities which are still shaped by continued unitedstatesian police power. This incongruity of cultural and political spaces makes of the 'border area', aptly named as such, an ambiguous zone. It is in this border area that identities are assigned and taken, withheld and rejected. The state seeks a monopoly on the power to assign identities to those who enter this space. (58)

Kearney explains the complex contestation of the border zone from both sides. Even though the US might be the more influential party in the control and policing of borders, it is equally possible to "reconquer" some of the territory demarcated by the establishment of borders. As a result of this contestation, there is an "incongruity of cultural and political spaces". In the Indian context, Ghosh chooses to represent the example of the grandmother's experience and perception of borders in *The Shadow Lines*. Her perception is of course shaped by her commitment to the Indian nation state that she helped to build in the struggle for independence. Her generation of nationalists is confronted with the continuous changes of the nation state and therefore it is more difficult to accept and truly understand the differences between the new nations emerging on the Indian subcontinent. Her expectations to be able to *see* the border between India and East Pakistan as an actual visible line of demarcation is a case in point. While her perceptions highlight the abstract and arbitrary nature of national borders, the death of Tridib, the narrator's cousin, is a painfully concrete consequence of the border's violent history. In his death, the contrast between perceived space and the real consequence of the establishment of borders finally culminate. Tridib, the experienced traveller and citizen of the world, becomes the victim of inter-religious violence that again and again erupts between the increasingly more antagonistic Hindus and Muslims, an antagonism born from the idea of the homogeneity of the nation in the course of Indian Independence and Partition.

4. *The Hungry Tide*: Precariousness of Life in the Sunderban Region

In *The Hungry Tide*, Ghosh does not abandon the historical power of spatial segregation and division, but adds environmentalist and human rights issues to his repertoire. In *The*

Hungry Tide, Ghosh's first outright ecocritical novel,[3] precariousness lies both in the socio-political organisation *and* in the natural environment. Ghosh tells the story of the young biologist Pyia who arrives in the Sunderbans, a region shaped by the enormous Ganges delta that opens up into the Bay of Bengal, where she plans to study a rare type of river dolphin. A parallel plot centres on Kanai, a young translator from Delhi. Both characters are newcomers to the region and are gradually familiarised with the difficulties of the local settlers and their precarious co-existence with the forces of nature and harassment by the government. One of the main threats to human existence is the ever-changing natural habitat of the vast Ganges delta:

> There are no borders here to divide fresh water from salt, river from sea. The tides reach as far as two hundred miles inland and every day thousands of acres of forest disappear underwater, only to reemerge hours later. The currents are so powerful as to reshape the islands almost daily – some days the water tears away entire promontories and peninsulas; at other times it throws up new shelves and sandbanks where there were none before. (6-7)

The indeterminacy of the tide country makes it almost impossible, or at least extremely laborious, to settle there. Humans are in constant battle with the natural elements in order to secure their survival. Their precarious existence is further endangered by the wildlife on the islands as "[e]very year, dozens of people perish in the embrace of that dense foliage, killed by tigers, snakes and crocodiles" (7). Geographically as well as symbolically, this indeterminate space functions as a setting that naturally generates stories of struggle, survival and suffering, yet the narrative includes the socio-political impact on this space to make it clear that human existence is always shaped by the complex interrelationships between the geographical and the social aspects of space.

The history of the island settlement is introduced in several passages giving an insight into the changing conditions for the islanders:

> Despite its small size, the island of Lusibari supported a population of several thousand. Some of its people were descended from the first settlers, who had arrived in the 1920s. Others had come in successive waves, some after the partition of the subcontinent of 1947 and some after the Bangladesh war of 1971. Many had come even more recently, when other nearby islands were forcibly depopulated in order to make room for wildlife conservation projects. (50)

The islands of the Sunderbans, as becomes clear in several of such short informative passages, are both refuge in times of war and sites of continuous removal and dislocation. The waves of refugees settling there in the course of the twentieth century cannot consider this region as a safe space or home for longer periods of time. Spatial regula-

[3] In their introduction to postcolonial ecocriticism, Huggan and Tiffin state that the "environmental imagination" after Buell utilised "a set of aesthetic preferences for ecocriticism which is not necessarily restricted to environmental realism or nature writing, but is especially attentive to those forms of fictional and non-fictional writing that highlight nature and natural elements (landscape, flora fauna, etc.) as self-standing agents, rather than support structures for human action, in the world" (13).

tions that turn the islands into conservation projects overlook the needs of the humans who have only settled there to escape war as well as political or religious persecution. The novel does more than document the fate of the islanders: it tells a comprehensive and inclusive history of the region as the narrative combines the aspects of an ecocritical text, a biological discourse on the rare species of river dolphins as well as the difficult co-existence of humans and tigers in the conservation areas, and additionally the portrayal of the endeavours of social projects to improve life on the islands. In order to avoid a complete fragmentation of these individual aspects, the story is centred on a few representative characters, with the young biologist at the core.

The Hungry Tide starts out with the return of Piya, who is of Indian origin and was educated in the US, to the Sunderban region. After initial problems to find a local guide, Piya finds a good companion in Fokir, a lower-caste fisherman whose capacities help her to locate the habitat of the rare species. Piya's character transports a set of values such as Western science, rationality, environmentalism and emancipation that are confronted with the values and culture of the Sunderban region. Despite the fact that she is used to fend for herself, Piya begins to trust Fokir's indigenous knowledge of his surroundings and even without the help of verbal communication is able to depend and learn from him, becoming, at the same time, emotionally attached.

Apart from telling the story of Piya and Fokir, the novel consists of passages that include the voice of Nirmal, a leftist intellectual and writer who settled in Lusibari with his wife in the 1950s. His diary, which is given to Kanai, his nephew, after his death, tells the story around the Morichjhapi incident, revealing how the settlers first opposed the repressions and plans of deportation by the government under the regulations of the Forest Preservation Act. Although the story is not completely recounted and leaves out the violent end of the besieged island, namely how its inhabitants were attacked, killed and deported, it nevertheless gives a glimpse of the islanders' resistance. This fragment of the island's history would have been lost if Nirmal's diary had not been saved. Even such a personal and inconclusive narrative as the unfinished diary provides an insight into the precariousness of a group of people that in Butler's terms is more "subject to arbitrary violence than others" (xii).

Next to Nirmal's diary, another discourse about the Ganges delta can be regarded as a response to the natural environment and a strategy of survival. The inhabitants of the tide country take comfort in the legends that encircle the Ganges delta:

> In our legends it is said that the Goddess Ganga's descent from the heavens would have split the earth had Lord Shiva not tamed her torrent by tying it into his ash-smeared locks. To hear this story is to see the river in a certain way: as a heavenly braid, for instance, an immense rope of water, unfurling through a wide and thirsty plain. That there is a further twist to the tale becomes apparent only in the final stages of the river's journey – and this part of the story always comes as a surprise, because it is never told and thus never imagined. It is this: there is a point at which the braid becomes undone; where Lord Shiva's matted hair is washed apart into a vast knotted tangle. Once past that point the river throws off its bindings and separates into hundreds, maybe thousands, of tangled strands. (6)

If one reads carefully, the passage reveals that even the legend cannot grasp, or adequately describe, the river delta.[4] Even though the legend claims that the god Shiva tames the goddess Ganga by tying her into his hair, "the braid becomes undone" when the river finally arrives in the delta region where it "separates into hundreds, maybe thousands, of tangled strands". Ghosh seems to suggest here that the indeterminate space, the in-between space of land, river and sea, does not have a corresponding legendary story to render it more comprehensible. Even though the space often generates stories and legends since, as Gurr argues, "the text's narrative and ecological concerns are interwoven [and] the entire plot literally grows out of the fundamental characteristics of the landscape" (70), the unsteady nature of the river delta cannot be captured in language. It is perhaps the victory of the braid, the torrent over the god, which makes this story too disturbing to be told. In the tide country, the river actually does split the earth and spills out into the sea, thus opening up the land to the vastness of the ocean, a true triumph over Lord Shiva. Even myths and legends cannot in fact truly represent the precariousness of the natural environment.

The Hungry Tide does not only tell the legends of its region but juxtaposes different forms of knowledge about the natural habitat. Piya's work as a marine biologist as well as her Western education frame her understanding as much as the legends and myths are a source of knowledge for the villagers. Fokir, moreover, embodies the practical everyday knowledge of a fisherman who is said to feel more at home on his boat than on land. While Piya uses maps and technical devices for orientation, Fokir's knowledge of his surroundings must somehow rely on a radically different notion of space. Even though Ghosh gives us detailed descriptions of Piya's equipment and her scientific expertise as a biologist,[5] Fokir's resource of knowledge remains undocumented and opaque. The novel's depiction is limited to this:

> By this time the fog had thinned and with the tide at its lowest ebb, the shore was revealed to be no more than a few hundred feet away. Piya saw that Fokir had stopped the boat at a point where the shore curved like the inside of an arm, creating a long patch of unperturbed water in the crook of the river's elbow. (95-96)

We witness how Fokir takes Piya to the requested point in the river where she can observe the rare species of river dolphin, but the text does not give us any clues as to Fokir's navigational skills and knowledge of the animal's habitat. Passages that highlight the character's behaviour are rendered from the point of view of Piya and thus preclude the reader from getting access to Fokir's thoughts. It is interesting that Ghosh does not give the reader information on Fokir's knowledge of the natural environment and whether his familiarity with the river, its dangerous rhythm of ebb and tide and the

[4] Lord Shiva is, especially in contrast to Vishnu, seen as the more threatening and ambiguous god. The ambiguity of his character is due to the common view of him as both benign and dangerous (Bansal 37).

[5] Piya's expertise and credentials as a scientist are underlined by the detailed description of her technical equipment: "Along with the GPS monitor was a rangefinder and a depth sounder, which could provide an exact reading of the water's depth when its sensor was dipped beneath the surface" (62).

animals that inhabit the tide country, is instinctive or learned, inherited or studied. It is paradoxically Fokir, the man who seems closer to nature than any other character, who dies in a storm while protecting Piya from it. His knowledge of the tide country with its perilous and indeterminable changes does not save him. It is Piya who survives and, perhaps rather ironically, records the routes that Fokir has shown her in the river delta on her portable GPS device so that his knowledge is saved for posterity through the means of technology.[6]

Ghosh's preoccupation with precarious space(s) in *The Hungry Tide* is an element that further complements the set of spatial representations and considerations of *The Shadow Lines*. Nature and the natural habitat of both animals and humans in the eco-system of the tide country are well-chosen for the central setting and spatial constellation Ghosh puts under scrutiny here. Whether it is indeed what Huggan and Tiffin call a "post-imperial concept of community" (6) that the novel suggests as an alternative to the mutual killings of humans and animals in the Sunderbans remains open, yet Ghosh draws attention to the difficult relationship between the human and animal species. When Piya is horrified by the villagers' brutal killing of a tiger who is first captured and then burnt alive in a cage, Kanai puts forth the argument that Western environmentalism is complicit with the hostility that exists between people and wildlife in this region:

> 'Because it was people like you', said Kanai, 'who made a push to protect the wildlife here, without regard for the human costs. And I'm complicit because people like me – Indians of my class, that is – have chosen to hide these costs, basically in order to curry favour with their Western patrons. It's not hard to ignore the people who're dying – after all, they are the poorest of the poor.' (248-249)

Through the figure of Kanai, a Westernised urban middle-class Indian man, Ghosh presents a critique of imperialist forms of government that exclude the indigenous population since they favour and protect the interests of a one-sided environmentalism instead. The novel does not make any concrete suggestions how to solve this situation but instead opens up a dialogue between the different standpoints. The environmentalist and biologist Piya begins to re-think her position and Fokir is confronted with Piya's rejection of the killing of tigers, while Kanai also learns about the problems of the region and during his stay in the Sunderbans looses his urban middle-class aloofness and arrogance.

[6] In an interview with Claire Chambers, Ghosh talks about the importance of conversations, the influence of the leading figure in psychoanalysis in India, Ashis Nandy, and, perhaps more pertinently to my argument here, his interest in science, both Indian and Western science and the difference between those. He furthermore points out that science and more generally knowledge – Western and Indian forms of knowledge – are subjects that he is very much devoted to. Not only does he examine different types of knowledge and scientific discourses but he also looks at the ways in which knowledge is recorded and made available, whereby some discourses occlude the voices on the margins (Chambers 31).

5. Conclusion

While *The Shadow Lines* is set within the theoretical framework of history and narrative in both colonial and postcolonial contexts,[7] *The Hungry Tide*, as we have seen, definitely marks a shift to spatial narrative with a decidedly ecocritical viewpoint. One of the major concerns of postcolonial ecocriticism is the systematic colonisation of both land and its people under colonialism. What postcolonial and ecocritical theories share is the critique of the violent usurpation of indigenous land, subjecting both the human and non-human inhabitants to the logic of Western progress and capitalism. The dichotomy of Western and non-Western social forms and their impact on the environment is summed up by Huggan and Tiffin with reference to the ecofeminist Val Plumwood:

> As Plumwood argues, the western definition of humanity depended – and still depends – on the presence of the 'not-human': the uncivilised, the animal and animalistic. European justification for invasion and colonisation proceeded from this basis, understanding non-European lands and the people and animals that inhabited them as 'spaces, unused, under-used or empty'. (5)

When humans are turned into the primitive, into something more like space, then it is vital for a critique of colonial regimes and their ideology to uncover the mechanisms underneath these forms of dehumanisation and how they might still operate in postcolonial societies. As a point of convergence one may take the conceptualisation of the human versus the non-human in order to establish a clearer picture of the hierarchies that are at work in particular regions and environments. Along those lines, Huggan and Tiffin suggest that

> a re-imagining and reconfiguration of the human place in nature necessitates an interrogation of the category of the human itself and of the ways in which the construction of ourselves *against* nature – with the hierarchisation of life forms that construction implies – has been and remains complicit in colonialist and racist exploitation from the time of imperial conquest to the present day. (6)

It is precisely such a "hierarchisation of life forms" that Ghosh questions in his oeuvre. The novels discussed above exemplify how such hierarchies are tied to different spatial dimensions (physical, social and mental) that shape human precariousness. One might claim that precariousness in postcolonial contexts, as Ghosh's novels make clear, can only be understood in spatial terms if one considers the consequences of drawing and re-drawing maps. But I would suggest that Ghosh's novels go further than other post-

[7] It is interesting to note that Ghosh himself stated in an interview that he finds the term "postcolonial" rather problematic: "I have no truck with this term at all. […] It completely misrepresents the focus of the work that I do. In some really important ways, colonialism is not what interests me. What is postcolonial? When I look at the work of critics, such as Homi Bhabha, I think they have somehow invented this world which is just a set of representations of representations. They've retreated into a world of magic mirrors and I don't think anyone can write from that sort of position" (qtd. in Chambers 37).

colonial novels which – like Salman Rushdie's *Midnight's Children* (1981) – create a national, pan-Indian narrative, by showing the local and regional specificities of the Indian-Pakistani and Indian-Bangladeshi contestations of space. Without an in-depth analysis of the spatial narratives of embattled regions such as the border zones and contested boundaries of nations in *The Shadow Lines* or the Sunderbans in *The Hungry Tide*, the precariousness of its inhabitants – both humans and animals – might easily be overlooked. Therefore, I have suggested that Ghosh invests in the careful description of physical, social and mental space with its impact on subjective and historically shifting notions of national and regional identity. Often these national and regional identities are under threat by wars and ethnic conflicts, yet another force comes into play when precariousness is caused by nature. As a response to this kind of precariousness, one that is increasingly of greater concern in postcolonial literature, Ghosh's narratives give an insight into local knowledge of nature and culture without giving precedence to either animals or humans but rather their necessarily shared habitats.

Works Cited

Azaryahu, Maoz, and Kenneth E. Foote. "Historical Space as Narrative Medium: On the Configuration of Spatial Narratives of Time at Historical Sites." *GeoJournal* 73.3 (2008): 179-194. Retrieved 11 Aug. 2013. <http://wyoshpo.state.wy.us/pdf/azaryahu.spatialnarrative-final.pdf>.

Bansal, Sunita Pant. *Hindu Gods and Goddesses*. Noida: Smriti Books, 2005.

Black, Shameem. "Cosmopolitanism at Home: Amitav Ghosh's *The Shadow Lines*." *Journal of Commonwealth Literature* 41.3 (2006): 45-65.

Butler, Judith. *Precarious Life: The Powers of Mourning and Violence*. London and New York: Verso, 2004.

Carter, Paul. *The Road to Botany Bay: An Essay in Spatial History*. London: Faber, 1987.

Chambers, Claire. "The Absolute Essentialness of Conversations: A Discussion with Amitav Ghosh." *Journal of Postcolonial Writing* 41.1 (2005): 26-39.

Ghosh, Amitav. *The Hungry Tide*. New York: Houghton Mifflin, 2005.

—. *The Shadow Lines*. 1988. New Delhi: Ravi Dayal, 1998.

Gurr, Jens Martin. "Emplotting an Ecosystem: Amitav Ghosh's *The Hungry Tide* and the Question of Form in Ecocriticism." *Local Natures, Global Responsibilities: Ecocritical Perspectives on the New English Literatures*. Ed. Laurenz Volkmann et al. Amsterdam and New York: Rodopi, 2010. 69-80.

Huggan, Graham, and Helen Tiffin. *Postcolonial Ecocriticism: Literature, Animals, Environment*. London and New York: Routledge, 2009.

Kearney, Michael. "Borders and Boundaries of State and Self at the End of Empire." *Journal of Historical Sociology* 4.1 (1991): 52-74.

Lefebvre, Henri. *The Production of Space*. 1974. Trans. Donald Nicholson-Smith. Oxford: Blackwell, 1991.

Mallot, J. Edward. "'A Land Outside Space, an Expanse without Distances': Amitav Ghosh, Kamila Shamsie and the Maps of Memory." *Literature Interpretation Theory* 18.3 (2007): 261-284.

Neilson, Brett, and Ned Rossiter. "From Precarity to Precariousness and Back Again: Labour, Life and Unstable Networks." *The Fibreculture Journal* 5 (2005). Retrieved 11 Aug. 2013. <http://journal.fibreculture.org/issue5/neilson_rossiter_print.html>.

Soja, Edward. *Postmodern Geographies: The Reassertion of Space in Critical Social Theory.* London and New York: Verso, 1989.

Part Two

Precarious Selves

Stephan Laqué

Cynicism and the Fringes of the Human: Mike Leigh's *Naked*

Apart from giving us some of the best-known British films of the last decades, director Mike Leigh has also firmly established a cultural trope. A Mike Leigh film is always recognizably a Mike Leigh film, with humble domestic settings where subdued and benign characters from the lower middle-class lead their typically dismal and damaged lives. That memorable and quintessentially British line by Pink Floyd, "hanging on in quiet desperation is the English way",[1] perfectly captures setting, plot, characters and mood of these films. There is a sameness to Leigh's work which, according to the man himself, circles around "things like work, surviving, having an aged parent or whether it's a good idea to have kids" (qtd. in Fuller xxi). Indeed, current derogatory remarks about him being a "kitchen-sink realist" or a "council-estate realist" (Watson 17)[2] may ring true – until one watches his masterwork *Naked* of 1993. As I want to show in this chapter, the special form of precariousness which this film explores is less to do with financial or social difficulties, but with *parrhesia*, with that compulsive form of self-exposure which is the mark of the cynic.

Though also set on the lower rungs of the social ladder, *Naked* is neither kitchen-sink nor council-flat – and it is markedly less realist than the rest of Leigh's oeuvre. Though filmed exclusively on location, the film appears stylized and at times artful almost to the point of seeming artificial. One important reason for this unexpected flavour is Leigh's use of the bleach bypass process (Fuller xxxix) which renders colours more saturated. Importantly, however, the film shows oversaturation not just of colour, but also, as it were, of character. The central character of *Naked* is called Johnny, a restless mid-twenties intellectual from Manchester who is on the dole, on the streets and on the run. He is oversaturated in his cleverness and his boldness; oversaturated in the way in which he is at once endearing and obnoxious, vulnerable and violent. Johnny – who is masterfully played by David Thewlis – is a slim and emaciated figure clad in black. With a boyishly full head of hair above black shirt, black coat, black Levi's and black Doc Marten's shoes, he looks like the stereotype of the disgruntled teenager – but Johnny's discontent is more substantial than any juvenile self-fashioning. It is not simply more mature, but more substantial, more fundamental. He combines the sophistication and erudition of a public-school education with the austerity and aggression of the street. Johnny is therefore less a character than an experiment, a study in the extremes to which human nakedness in the sense of self-exposure can be pushed.

The pre-title sequence which starts the film is nothing if not disturbing. A very unsteady steadycam is raced up a dark alley where Johnny and an older woman are, as the

[1] The line is from the song "Time" on the 1973 Pink Floyd album *Dark Side of the Moon*.

[2] Gary Watson fervently rejects these categories.

script has it, “having a rough fuck under a streetlamp” (Leigh 5). As the woman’s moans and her “come on” change into cries of pain and a whimpering “you’re hurting me”, it becomes clear that this “rough fuck” has, in fact, turned into a rape. Both Mike Leigh and his leading actor David Thewlis have rejected an interpretation of the scene as rape, with Thewlis saying that “[a]t the beginning, that’s not a rape. It’s sex that gets out of hand. That’s not to condone it. Obviously he’s out of order” (qtd. in Watson 16). However, it is important that this “getting out of hand” be not construed as a gradual and merely quantitative shift, but that it is allowed to cause a categorical change: sex turns into rape. The scene starts with sex and ends with rape and this, needless to say, constitutes a big difference. This is importantly a keeling over of the action, a loss of balance for which there can be no possible moral justification. Indeed, the question of keeping the balance and of tilted balances becoming destructive and inimical to life is central to the film and, above all else, central to its protagonist Johnny. Using the scene of a rape at the beginning in order to convey this agenda may come across as a fairly crude device designed to shock rather than to illustrate or explain, but for all its subtlety, depth and cultivation, *Naked* is a raw brute of a film which clubs you over the head and leaves you stunned.

The shaky tracking shot into the alley which starts the film takes the audience straight into Johnny’s unsteady life, into the dark and seedy recesses of the world and of the mind where it takes place. The shot also conveys a good sense of the driven nature of Johnny’s existence and it drives him further along. Having escaped Johnny’s clutches, the woman screams: “I’m gonna tell my Bernard of you!! You’re fucking dead!!” (Leigh 5). Bent over and turned away from the woman, Johnny beats the air in exasperation – an exasperation which, as the film will show, is not directed at the woman or her belligerent boyfriend, but at himself. Johnny’s agonized contortion shows how keenly yet helplessly he is aware of things in his life “getting out of hand”: he runs off, steals a car and as the titles roll we see him driving over empty night-time motorways towards London, the ineluctable movement perfectly underlined by Andrew Dickson’s fast-paced musical score. This sinister sense of compulsion is something that will carry Johnny through the entire film, through a series of intellectual encounters – some verbal, some also painfully physical – on to his inevitable centrifugal escape from London which reverses his centripetal drive south at the start.

Johnny is driven to move down to London, around London and again away to wherever, but he is, above all else, driven to talk. An unremitting stream of witticisms, puns, banalities, insights, trivia, put-downs, nuggets of sheer genius as well as any number of verbal attacks indiscriminately directed at each and everyone he encounters pours from his mouth during his aimless peregrinations. To Johnny, any sense of direction is to be mocked. When in one of the first dialogues of the film his friend Louise asks him by what means of transport he got to London, he describes his irruption into her world in a characteristically caustic send-up of the compulsive and disorderly process of evolution:

> Well, basically... There was this little dot, right? And the dot went bang and the bang expanded, energy formed into matter, matter cooled, matter lived, the amoeba the fish, the fish the fowl, the fowl the froggy, the froggy the mammal, the mammal the monkey, the monkey the man. *Amo, amas, amat, quid pro quo, memento mori, ad infinitum*, sprinkle on a bit of grated cheese and leave under the grill till Doomsday. (11-12)

There is a seamless transition here from the evolution of mankind to the supposed progress of and through language indicated by the litany of verb forms from a Latin primer from where Johnny pushes his tirade on to an arbitrary scatter of Latin phrases and a 'recipe' which reduces the grand scheme of things to a clichéd and quite irrelevant domestic footnote. Here as everywhere in the film, Johnny is a far cry from the "quiet desperation" found in other Mike Leigh films. His desperation is very much language-based. On the one hand, it is continuously articulated, on the other, it is founded on his constant punning exploration of language, of contradictions, inconsistencies and semantic spillover. This obsessive engagement with language does not even stop in one of the most intimate moments of the film when Sophie, the punk flatmate of his erstwhile girlfriend Louise, places his hand inside her bra: "Oh. Thanks for the mammaries" (17). I would like to argue that this compulsive talking and quarrelling shows Johnny to be a cynic and that by exploring the precarious life of this particular cynic, the film offers a critique of the derogatory stereotype of "cynical postmodernism".[3]

Mike Leigh himself has vehemently rejected the notion that Johnny is cynical: "one of the most naïve things that have been said about him is that he's cynical. He's not cynical. He's sceptical about some things but he has a sense of values. At the same time he can't cope with actual relationships. These contradictions fascinated me" (qtd. in Fuller xxxv). I beg to differ. The contradictions which Leigh is talking about are, in fact, precisely part and parcel of what Michel Foucault has defined as cynical philosophy. While Johnny may not be cynical in the broad colloquial sense of being narcissistically wilful and pointlessly antagonistic, he is still quite unmistakably a cynic. The very title of the film – *Naked* – is pointing in this direction. As Foucault writes in his lecture series *The Government of Self and Others*, a cynic "is someone who does not seek to conceal his desires, passions, dependencies, etcetera, but who presents himself naked, in his destitution" (347). Johnny does not hide. He may run away from the wrath of some irate Bernard in Manchester, but when towards the end of the film he gives the closest thing to an answer he can provide to the question of his motivation for coming to London, he explains that "I 'ad to get out of Manchester 'cos I was gonna get a beatin'. And I come down 'ere and, er… get a beatin'" (Leigh 87). Adversity is part of the cynic's life – in Manchester as well as in London. What according to Foucault causes the ineluctable beating which the cynic brings upon himself is *parrhesia*, the compulsion to say everything, to speak one's mind and to speak the truth regardless of the consequences. Foucault describes the scope of this principle:

> When you accept the *parrhestiastic* game in which your own life is exposed, you are taking up a specific relationship to yourself: you risk death to tell the truth instead of reposing in the security of a life where the truth goes unspoken. [...] In *parrhesia*, the speaker uses his freedom and chooses frankness instead of persuasion, truth instead of falsehood or silence, the risk of death instead of life and security, criticism instead of flattery, and moral duty instead of self-interest and moral apathy. [...] Philosophical

[3] Timothy Bewes has offered a comprehensive genealogy and critique of this cliché. However, his definition of cynicism as "a melancholic, self-pitying reaction to the apparent disintegration of political reality (in the form of 'grand narratives' or 'totalizing ideologies')" (7) does not take into account the genuinely radical and driven nature of the cynical mindset.

> *parrhesia* is thus associated with the theme of the care of oneself (*epimeleia heautou*). (*Fearless Speech* 17-24)

Parrhesia is not just an activity or even an obligation. It is the governing principle by which the cynic shapes his entire life. Nakedness and self-exposure lie paradoxically at the heart of his "care for himself". The cynic does not care for his own safety, but for his own exposure, for his own precariousness. Leading a precarious life is what being a cynic is all about – and as Foucault claims, this is an attitude which has been lost since antiquity: "Throughout Antiquity philosophy is really lived as the free questioning of men's conduct by a truth-telling which accepts the risk of danger to itself. To that extent it seems to me that the most typical form of ancient philosophy is that [of] the Cynic" (*Government of Self* 346).

Johnny is indeed a cynic, but for all his classical reading, he is surely not a straightforward resuscitation of a lost ancient ideal.[4] His *parrhesia* is postmodern in that his attacks are directed against the almost metaphysically all-encompassing boredom, indifference and ignorance which he encounters everywhere. He therefore sets out to subvert others' faith in certainty and coherence – all in a playful but thoroughly serious way which derives its force from an exceptionally quick-witted and astute handling and manipulation of language. Johnny's attitude is what in his otherwise famously flawed description of postmodernism Leslie Fiedler has fortuitously called "joyous misology" (33), a gleeful and enthusiastic contempt for intellectual complacency. The truth which Johnny promulgates in order to counter this complacency is the impossibility of truth and the untenability of confidence and hope. What he ends up conveying to his interlocutors is a sense of his own precarious life.

The first person Johnny meets in London is Sophie, whom Johnny proceeds to treat to the first of his many tirades:

> Johnny: Would you describe yourself as a happy little person?
> Sophie: Yeah... I'm the life and soul.
> Johnny: Have you ever thought, right... I mean, you don't know, but you might already 'ave had the happiest moment in your whole fuckin' life, and all you've got to look forward to is sickness and purgatory?
> Sophie: Oh shit! Well... I just live from day to day, meself.
> Johnny: I tend to skip a day now and again – you know what I mean? (Leigh 9)

Though clearly not a positive thinker, Johnny is certainly not a nihilist either. His rhetoric follows an almost pedagogic aim: to subvert complacency, along with its more pleasant companions hope and happiness. The stability of a happy life – the "life and

[4] The classical reading which Johnny explicitly demonstrates in the film is epic rather than philosophical. When a young waitress ill-advisedly invites him back to the flat she is watching for a gay couple, he comments on the books on their shelves: "No, I don't mean that to sound... homerphobic. I mean, I like *The Iliad*. And *The Odyssey*. (*Laughs*.) D'you get that?" (Leigh 63). As I am arguing, Johnny's Homeric journey through London is motivated by the very un-Homeric force of *parrhesia* – no return home, but rather a denial of the centredness and safety which a home implies.

soul" – simply does not fit into his order of things. Johnny's thinking is far less orderly and smooth. In jerks and bouts of free association it typically follows a downward spiral. The comfort of living or thinking coherently in a stable movement "from day to day" is therefore something he has to tear apart with the odd notion of "skipping a day now and again".

As far as anyone watching the film can tell, Johnny is poor. We see him leaving a humble front door in Manchester on his way to London, so we can infer that at least he has a home of some kind. Together with Sophie he professes to being on the dole, unlike Louise who has got a "posh job in the big shitty" (14). Being naked and without a job are important parts of Johnny's "care of himself" as a cynic. He is therefore not the product of poverty;[5] rather, poverty is a necessary adjunct to his special brand of *parrhesia*. Seeing the film as a work of social criticism, as a rejection of the dismal post-Thatcher era of British conservatism, is thus a reductive (though possible) reading. But the thrust of the film is far more fundamental than a statement about or against social disadvantage. Apart from being economically precarious, the life it represents is in flux, constantly losing its own balance and upsetting that of its surroundings. The cynic is at the mercy of a world which is perfectly justified in seeing him as a threat. Jonathan Romney, an early reviewer, said that watching *Naked* was "like being trapped for two hours in a railway carriage with a charismatic preacher who might possibly have an axe under his coat" (qtd. in Watson 15). This assessment is very apt indeed, only that the axe is out in the open in the ever-present stream of aspersions which Johnny is casting at everything and everyone.

With what I take to be a touch of tongue-in-cheek irony, Leigh has claimed that the film is, in fact, "about the impending apocalypse" (qtd. in Fuller xxxviii). It would be hard to reconcile this notion with the open-ended and largely plotless structure of the film which, nonetheless, does conjure up images of and apprehensions about the apocalypse in a number of places. Still, nothing in the film ever moves towards the kind of closure which the apocalypse would entail. The apocalypse is never impending, but it is a trope which both the film and its protagonist use throughout in order to combat "the fatal indifference of modern man" (Coveney 33).[6] This theme and device is particularly in evidence in the centre of the film. When on the day after his arrival Louise gets home from work, Johnny restlessly moves around the house – followed by Sophie who has

[5] Ray Carney and Leonard Quart have noted that Leigh refrains from reducing characters in this way: "The film never suggests that the advent of a measure of social justice and equality could transform the lives of characters like Sophie or Brian. Leigh avoids reducing Johnny's behavior to a set of political and social variables or treating it as merely a manifestation of a social problem. It is Johnny the individual, not Johnny the homeless social victim or member of a displaced working-class intelligentsia, who is terrified of making personal commitments and incapable of using his powerful intelligence and literate wit in a productive way. The responsibility for his self-destructive behavior is not reductively arrogated to Thatcher, to capitalist greed and exploitation, or even to the inequities of the English class system" (237).

[6] However, Michael Coveney thinks that Johnny only cries out against indifference without doing anything about it: "He is crying out against the fatal indifference of modern man but he's not doing anything about it. He's just trying to get people to see what's going on, which is what the film will hopefully do" (33). I would argue that, on the contrary, crying out is the most effective action he can possibly take.

helplessly fallen for his oblique boyish charm. Exasperated by Louise's imperviousness to his attacks and irritated by Sophie's neediness which threatens to pin him down, his movements become more and more frantic until he is centrifugally, as it were, hurled into the night. He walks the streets and eventually sits down outside a closed shop where he notices a young unkempt Scot shouting "Maggie!", grunting and uncontrollably twitching his head. Archie (the name of the illiterate young man) is on the run from the police after smashing his father's head in with a poker and is looking for his girlfriend Maggie. Archie and Maggie are the only properly homeless people in the film and Johnny immediately adopts an almost paternal attitude to this grotesquely derelict and lost couple. He buys food for Maggie and tries to help them find each other. This mellowness is surprising and it seems that it is Johnny's subtle way of upsetting the world of those whose world has already utterly fallen to pieces. After some irrelevant jokes at the cost of the uncomprehending Scot – "D'you dream in Scotch? [...] Like, dream about sporran-clad, caber-tossin' haggis, gallopin' over porridge-covered glens?" (Leigh 28) – Johnny tries to provoke a reaction by offering a debate about Nostradamus, the apocalypse and self-fulfilling prophecy, but to no avail. Archie seems to be speaking a foreign language which contains little besides the words 'fuck' and 'cunt' and assorted snorts and grunts. Outside language Johnny cannot operate, and so he sends Archie away only to meet Maggie who is equally broken – but at least speaks English. Rather than Nostradamus, he treats her to a look into the abyss of London:

> Johnny: D'you not get like a sense of, like, a whole other world underneath all this? You know, like the guts of London? What with all the tube trains and everything, the city's viscera and the subterranean fuckin' fistulas and conduits and colons and bunkers and dungeons and tombs an' all that? [...] Does that freak you out?
> Maggie: Nah. (33)

Unlike Archie, Maggie can follow Johnny's train of thought, but she genuinely resists the pull which Johnny tries to set in motion. In a bid to disorient her, Johnny makes the very same suggestion to her which he offered Archie before: "Listen, love. I've got this great idea. Why don't you 'ave a little wander round and go look for the wee lad, an' I'll wait 'ere. An' if 'e turns up, I'll keep 'im 'ere till you get back" (30-31). Though he is here starting to mess with the two Scots, he eventually refrains from sending them off on a wild goose-chase and just laughs to himself, maybe recalling the fun he would be having if these were the cynic's usual customers. The cynical exposure of unstable foundations cannot shake Maggie since what life she may be having or may have had has already lost its footing. The cynic cannot get through to those who are beyond boredom, indifference and despair. Chasing and kicking each other – the word 'fuck' is used no less than 20 times on a single page of script (35) – Maggie and Archie leave Johnny alone and, for once, silent in front of a disused factory. The Scottish couple are a striking example of social criticism: Archie's constant bellowing for "Maggie!" and Johnny's wry comment that "those days are over" (28) are an obvious reference to the unfulfilled promise of the Thatcher years. But Johnny's mission is not part of this agenda of social satire and Archie and Maggie are not the clients or indeed 'disciples' he seeks and needs. So he moves on.

The second encounter of Johnny in this central part of the film is with a security guard named Brian who guards an enormous and entirely empty office building. Johnny sits in front of the glass doors of the entrance reading the Bible and when Brian notices him, the former believes that he may have found a kindred spirit. Brian is himself a reader of the Bible and something of an amateur philosopher – at last a worthy client for Johnny. Brian is as different from Archie and Maggie as the ultra-modern and brightly lit building he is guarding is from the delapidated bridges and dark walls of the previous scene. The security guard gives Johnny the cue for changing from the focus on space in his speeches of the Archie segment to a concern with time:

> Brian: Have you got nowhere to go, then?
> Johnny: Yeah... I've got an infinite number of fuckin' places to go. The problem is, where you stay. (38)

Staying somewhere in the present is alien to Johnny's nature – a nature which may well be painful to him. He is "homeless" in a number of ways, but so is Brian, who pointlessly guards empty space in what Johnny describes as a "postmodernist gas-chamber" (38). Brian is convinced of having led an earlier life in a cottage on the Irish coast and he works in pursuit of his aim to retire to this idyllic spot. Johnny proceeds to attack the faith in temporal succession upon which Brian's plans rest:

> See, you're all pissed off with the present, Bri, and there's nothing wrong with the present. The present's fine. The present's perfect. The present's peachy-fuckin-creamy. The only thing wrong with the present is the bastard doesn't exist. Because the present is the future, and the future is the past. And it's all the same fuckin' bag of bones anyway. It's a constant process of comin' into bein' and passin' away, comin' into bein' and passin' away. [...] The end of the world is nigh, Bri. The game is up! (45)

Up to this point, Johnny has estranged every single person he has met apart from Sophie. But Brian enjoys the intellectual repartee and bids farewell to the arch-cynic with a hackneyed but sound piece of advice: "Don't waste your life" (57).

Neither the Scottish couple nor Brian are in any way converted by their encounter with Johnny or significantly shaken in the way they live and regard their lives. The outcome of these two scenes would therefore mean defeat for Johnny were it not for the fact that the cynic is not engaging in a competition, but following an inescapable urge to talk, to say everything, *parrhesia*. While the rewards of this form of life are negligible, the risks are high: rejection, pity and outright violence. Violence eventually comes to Johnny in the form of a man who sticks up posters and who offers him a lift. To Johnny, the man's patent indifference to what he is doing is intolerable: "So is this your job, or a nice little hobby you've got for yourself? You're a lovely mover" (72). Johnny is exasperated by the purposeful pragmatism and monosyllabic efficiency of the poster man – and he begins to rise to the challenge:

> Johnny: So 'ow much d'you earn for doin' this?
> Man: It's none of your fucking business.

> Johnny: I mean, is the pay as substantial as say, er, the wages of sin? You know what I mean? Are you with me? (72)

Unlike the poster man, Brian, the guard from the previous scene, had commanded something approaching respect from Johnny – not by virtue of his erudition and intelligence, but because of the fact that he was prepared to acknowledge and reflect on what he was doing. He showed Johnny the digital device which records his movement around the empty building:

> Brian: My existence at this very moment on this very spot is now trapped and recorded. Twenty-three moments, twenty-three sites, every hour. That's my job.
> Johnny: Well, could they not train a tall chimpanzee to do that? Or a small chimpanzee with a bigger gizmo?
> Brian: I expect they could... yes.
> Johnny: What's your name, son?
> Brian: Brian.
> Johnny: Hallo, Brian – Johnny. Well, Brian, congratulations! You have succeeded in convincin' me that you do 'ave the most tedious fuckin' job in England. (42)

Brian is very much unlike Johnny: he has got plans and dreams and faith, an occupation and a steady income. But much like Johnny, he is prepared to look at the futility and shallowness behind the world he lives in. Though he may not be a preacher of futility of Johnny's calibre, he could be described as an interested disciple. The poster man, on the other hand, though significantly closer to Johnny in questions of financial security and social standing, immediately antagonizes him because of his manifest reluctance to acknowledge the fact that sticking up posters is not an eminently meaningful activity. When the poster man begins to glue notes announcing the cancellation of concerts across posters by the rock group Therapy?, Johnny aggressively points out that this activity carries moral implications and that it is part of the intellectual and moral depletion he castigates:

> What is all this anyway? What are you doing? Cancel everythin'. In the beginning was the word and the word was CANCELLED. D'you get like satisfaction out of this? D'you think you're making a contribution? You're like sort of publicly promulgatin' vacuities? Are you with me?
> (*The* MAN *walks off briskly*.)
> Fuckin' hell!! [...]
> Oh, that's it! Blank it all out! Blank it all out till you just atrophy and die of fuckin' indifference! (73-74)

The man, whose stoic tolerance of Johnny we may well have begun to admire, proceeds to knee Johnny in the crotch and to kick him in the street. Asking an imaginary audience for permission to scream, Johnny is nearly run over by a car and moves up an alley which closely resembles the one where the initial sex-turned-rape-scene took place. Once again, Johnny's life has 'got out of hand'. While there would have been a certain justice in Bernard's beating Johnny up in Manchester and while we can certainly see why the poster man is led to vent some of his pent-up anger on Johnny, it is an unspecific group of youngsters who find him in the alley and who for no apparent reason beat him to a pulp. Johnny's constant overstepping of the mark is catching up with him everywhere. Since *parrhesia* is not a form of gaining control, but the principle of relinquishing safety and control, it is only consistent with Johnny's driven nature that the beatings which he receives 'get out of hand', too, beyond and in defiance of such notions as justice and causality.

Peter Sloterdijk, the chief critic of cynicism, which he sees as the dominant ailment of modern culture, describes it as "enlightened false consciousness", and as an inherently hypocritical attitude: "The modern mass cynic loses his individual sting and spares himself the risk of exposure. He has long since ceased to subject his eccentricity to the attention and mockery of others" (192). Contemporary cynicism according to Sloterdijk practices "a nakedness which no longer has an unmasking effect" (194) and is thus devoid of any critical impulse. As I hope to have shown, Johnny is diametrically opposed to this jaded modern cynic. He returns to cynicism its remorselessly unmasking thrust and its powerful "individual sting" – what Foucault would describe as its classical heritage. Johnny, the postmodern cynic, regains some of the relevance of his premodern forefathers. He does not shrink back from exposure, but brazenly explores not just the fringes of society, but the fringes of humanity. In the words of Michel Foucault, he practices "philosophy as way of life, as flagrant way of life, as perpetual manifestation of the truth" (*Government of Self* 346). Following the rigour of classical cynicism, Johnny leads a dangerous and naked life – a precarious life. The dynamics which informs his life and which exasperates his interlocutors is thus recognizably late-modern, if not, indeed, postmodern. However, the life which he leads is more narrowly cynical in that Johnny's disregard of ethical standards and his refusal to show respect for his interlocutors are a far cry from the almost altruistic welcome of the other which postmodern thought demands. By rejecting fulfilment in human relationships, Johnny egoistically protects his cynical nakedness.[7] The same musical score which accompanied his drive to London during the titles sequence is again used at the end to emphasize the way in which Johnny is driven to move on. He hobbles out of the house and out of the lives of people who care for him. This is the closing shot of the film: "JOHNNY *keeps going ... We cut to black*" (Leigh 95). Johnny is leaving behind Louise who has gone into work to hand in her notice in order to return with him to Manchester. This callousness and tangible immorality keeps our attitude towards the character of Johnny suspended between admiration and contempt, between empathy and revulsion – a suitably precarious response to a magnificent exploration of contemporary cynical life.

[7] Tony Whitehead interprets Johnny's eventual escape from his revived relationship with Sophie as an attempt to protect an unspecific sociophobic liberty: "Genuine love and compassion would penetrate his defences, threaten his independence, challenge his more antipathetic instincts about himself and the people around him" (110).

Works Cited

Bewes, Timothy. *Cynicism and Postmodernity*. London and New York: Verso, 1997.

Carney, Ray and Leonard Quart. *The Films of Mike Leigh: Embracing the World*. Cambridge: Cambridge University Press, 2000.

Coveney, Michael. *The World According to Mike Leigh*. London: Harper Collins, 1997.

Fiedler, Leslie. "Cross the Border – Close the Gap." *Postmodernism: A Reader*. Ed. Patricia Waugh. London: Edward Arnold, 1994. 31-48.

Foucault, Michel. *Fearless Speech*. Ed. Joseph Pearson. Los Angeles, CA: Semiotext(e), 2001.

—. *The Government of Self and Others*. Trans. Graham Burchell. Basingstoke: Macmillan, 2010.

Fuller, Graham. "Mike Leigh's Original Features: An Interview by Graham Fuller." *Naked and Other Screenplays*. London: Faber, 1995. vii-xli.

Leigh, Mike. *Naked*. London: Faber, 1994.

Naked. Dir. Mike Leigh. Prod. Simon Channing Williams. Perf. David Thewlis, Katrin Cartlidge and Lesley Sharp. Thin Man Films, 1993.

Sloterdijk, Peter. "Cynicism – The Twilight of False Consciousness." *New German Critique* 33 (1981): 190-206.

Watson, Garry. *The Cinema of Mike Leigh: A Sense of the Real*. London and New York: Wallflower Press, 2004.

Whitehead, Tony. *Mike Leigh*. Manchester: Manchester University Press, 2007.

Jagna Oltarzewska

Hearing Eminem

Eminem's biography, stage persona and prolific output are fraught with the paradoxes that attend any commercially successful narrativization of precarious life, whether it be musical, theatrical or literary. I use the expression 'precarious life' in a less philosophically charged sense than Judith Butler in her essay of the same name, but the issues raised by Eminem's insistent performance of his poverty-stricken and turbulent background are not entirely foreign to Butler's theme. Butler's essay deals with representation as constrained by imperialist ideology; specifically, the censorship of human suffering promoted by the US government and diligently enforced in media coverage of the war against Iraq. Her conclusions are pessimistic: "We cannot", she avers, "under contemporary conditions of representation, hear the agonized cry or be compelled by the face [of the Other]" (150). The capitalized Other destined for invisibility is as much the US soldier as the dying Iraqi civilian; the screening of maimed bodies carries a permanent risk of alienating public support for war by directing sympathy towards undesirable destinations. Reading Butler, one is forcefully reminded of Gayatri Spivak's negative response to the question "can the subaltern speak?", a classic statement turning precisely on the vexed issue of representation, understood in both aesthetic and legal senses. Spivak has argued forcefully – and influentially – that the voice of an Asian Other cannot be heard when inscribed into First World theoretical discourse. In the wake of Spivak, Butler reminds us of the powerful ideological constraints moulding the visible and the audible in contemporary public space; she demonstrates how easily testimony – written, visual, oral – continues to slip beneath the radar as Western theorists remain blind to their geopolitical positioning, and hegemonic regimes of framing determine both what we can see and "what we can hear", to quote the title of Butler's introductory essay.

Transitioning from such inaudible subjects to the global hip hop phenomenon that is Eminem is a delicate task, to say the very least. We cannot, surely, expand the notion of subalternity to include categories as disparate and historically remote from one another as Spivak's occluded subject – the self-immolating Hindu widow – Butler's unfilmed and therefore invisible war casualties, and a brazenly vocal, intensely mediatized figure who harnesses language with a vengeance in the globally disseminated musical form known as rap? If muteness enters into the very definition of subalternity, rap would appear to be its antithesis – an energetic, if politically ambivalent mode of counter-address, rooted in black American experience, hybridized through contact with Puerto Rican and Chicano cultures, and increasingly counting white musicians – most conspicuously Eminem – among its practitioners. In what sense, then, can the notion of 'precarious life' be made relevant to rap's *enfant terrible*? In what sense, if any, does Eminem embody or represent the vulnerabilities his songs so graphically describe? Is the pathos of his narratives eclipsed by his aggressive stance and inflammatory speech? When a rapper works personal history into his music, what form of attention does it seek and receive? Is the imaginative act of voicing one's experience proof against a social inattentiveness that only a funk beat, an obscene lyric, a lurid visual can momentarily excite? Is rap's message fatally compromised by its capacity, its readiness, to involve the listener at this level? Does commercial success sit easily with chronicles of failure, grinding poverty and a continued narrative emphasis on survival against the odds? A Forbes-listed celebrity hardly possesses the street credentials of an emergent subculture. A record of precarious life may not just be one that is silenced by dominant discursive formations;[1] it may be a tale of pain and exclusion that globalized circuits of reception are fated to mishear.

1. Autofictions

Many of Eminem's raps, if not most of them, are autofictions – songs that dramatize his artistic coming-of-age and chronicle his turbulent experience of celebrity – stories constrained or 'fictioned' by the generic requirements of reality rap and the aesthetic parameters of flow and rhyme scheme. Tricia Rose reminds us that rappers "speak with the voice of personal experience" (*Black Noise* 2), and theirs are typically stories of urban life at the margins, of precarious existence in a *milieu* of violence and deprivation – stories of debt and dispossession, crime and substance abuse, clashes with the police, 'beefs' or arguments with fellow rappers, cycles of bullying and revenge, struggles for recognition. Eminem draws heavily on these *topoi*, as well as paying his dues to the Janus-face of fame: the abject and obsessive undertow of fan culture, the deleterious effects of cult status on a private life, the thrills and dangers of paranoid infatuation with one's own legend. His raps are at once self-searching and attuned to a thoroughly commercialized culture that amplifies the mythical resonance of their content. It must be noted that Eminem's experience of precarious life provides textbook material for his art. Born in 1972 as Marshall Mathers to a seventeen-year-old unemployed mother and an absentee father, Eminem's early existence was blighted by deprivation, neglect, dysfunctional parenting and victimization. His childhood years were nomadic and unsettled, he and his mother eventually taking up residence in Warren, a predominantly white suburb of Detroit. He changed schools several times, underachieved, was bullied regularly, once so viciously that he fell into a coma. When his desire to rap cristallized into a career ambition, he dropped out of school and held down a series of low-paid jobs in factories and restaurant kitchens while honing his verbal skills in battles on the local rap circuits. The film *8 Mile* (2002), loosely based on Eminem's chequered start in hip hop, charts this early period. His rise to fame was quick after he came second in the Rap Olympics of 1997. Three albums, *The Slim Shady LP* (1999), *The Marshall Mathers LP* (2000) – both Grammy award winners – and the Grammy-nominated *The Eminem Show* (2002) sealed his reputation.

This meteoric rise could only presage a fall, which duly came, and took its heaviest toll when Eminem's best friend and fellow-rapper Proof met a violent death in 2006.

[1] The term is Foucault's (31-39).

Eminem faded into a twilight zone of medication-dependency (including a near-fatal overdose) and seclusion, from which he emerged after a spell in rehabilitation with the albums *Relapse* (2009) and *Recovery* (2010). The early years of this trajectory were punctuated by intense and well-publicized marital upheaval. Among the autofictions growing out of these experiences we might mention tracks like "Rock Bottom" (*Slim Shady*), a macabre chronicle of desperate poverty and its consequences; "The Way I Am" (*Marshall Mathers*), "Sing for the Moment" (*The Eminem Show*), "When I'm Gone" (*Curtain Call*),[2] pieces that dwell on the addictive, alienating lure of celebrity; and, finally, "Beautiful" (*Relapse*), a muted, plangent tale of depression and self-doubt recounted in the ruins of Michigan Central Station. Each of these songs is concerned with forms of social and corporeal vulnerability, from the enraged odd-jobber "broke as fuck", struggling to make ends meet on "dead-end jobs with lame pay", spiralling down into armed robbery ("Rock Bottom"), to the newly-famous rapper reflecting on the transmission of social violence and the pitfalls of notoriety: the tightrope walk of an artist under fire from the media for incendiary lyrics, pursued by the judiciary, adored by fans, vilified by 'haters', condemned for promoting violence despite his claim that rap is less an aggressive act than a "reflection" and "explanation" of such acts: "music is reflection of self/ We just explain it" ("Sing for the Moment").

This, of course, is a precarious claim to make. The brutal content of rap provides endless fuel for cause and effect arguments, a social obsession fostered by the media. Rap's adversarial style constantly lays it open to charges of instigating a violence which it purports to mirror. The stakes of this debate are delineated with clarity in Tricia Rose's *The Hip Hop Wars*. Reflecting on the role of violence in rap, Rose advances various hypotheses, framed as so many questions: do incendiary lyrics celebrate violence? Are they a form of 'anger management', acts of self-healing through uncensored speech? Does the rapper's tale gratuitously inject its own dose of violence into existing social tensions? Or is the narrative a natural offshoot of a *milieu* where threats and the acting-out of aggression are part of daily routine? Rose's final question goes to the heart of the matter: "At what point", she asks, "do stories that emanate from an overly violent day-to-day life begin to encourage and support that aspect of everyday life and undercut the communities' anti-violent efforts?" (*Hip Hop Wars* 55) It would be vain to suggest that the market success of the gangsta brand has no relevance here. Aggressive promotion and astronomical sales exert pressure on content, recycling those aspects of the tale that shock and titillate. Anger is the mandatory form of address; a raw affect suited to the expression of protest, it does not sit easily with repeated performance, all too often degenerating into a form of self-parodic smouldering ire. Eminem's tales of precarious life are wrathful accounts, but his is a wrath constructed artfully, with attention to pitch, intonation and strategic repetition – in "The Way I Am", the rap is delivered as one continuous, vindictive rant with insistent vocal emphasis on the long 'e' [ɪː]; a perfect illustration of Denise Riley's insight that "[r]age speaks monotonously" (53). In everyday speech situations, a tirade always teeters on the verge of bathos, while the diction of rage tends towards repetition, undermining the speaker's poise. On the face of it, wrath is an unpropitious vehicle for sustained narrative, though its very fragilities may recommend it in an account of precarious life. Eminem's fury is

2 Eminem's *Curtain Call: The Hits* is a compilation album released in 2005.

articulated with extreme vocal dexterity; this, and an inventive lyricism create powerful affect, an affect no longer tethered to the specifics of an originating moment, a particular body, an individual listening consciousness.[3] It prompts the listener to look beyond her visceral response and consider the forces promoting such vigorous production – and consumption – of rage.

2. Modes of Mishearing

I have suggested that Eminem's narratives may be misheard, and in what follows I would like to examine more closely what makes them singularly precarious records of precarious life. I will go on to propose a form of close listening which attempts to correlate Eminem's vitriolic narratives of private misery to a historical conjuncture – our own – a conjuncture they illuminate, and which, in turn, informs and broadens their meaning. We can distinguish several responses to Eminem, each of which remains deaf, in its own way, to the fine detail and broader import of his music. The first, alluded to above, is a form of distracted listening, similar in kind to Walter Benjamin's 'distracted attention' (cf. 232-234); by the mid-1930s, Benjamin's sensibilities had already been struck by the changing quality of reception commanded by art, and he noted the widespread tendency to observe "in a state of distraction" (232), a tendency which found a timely correlate in the development of the film medium. Today, as aural and visual stimuli increase exponentially, so the contemporary listener extracts those qualities which are salient but may be incidental; there is less and less time to devote undivided attention to a whole. Yet there is a great deal more to a rap song than beat, chorus and hook. Typically, Eminem's songs are longer than the average pop ballad, lasting over four minutes, some as long as five. Punning lyrics, complex rhyme schemes, verbal flow of varying speed, staccato delivery, strategic silences are played off against the beat, generating intricate effects of sense within a powerful, four beat to a bar structure. A listener will tend to retain a beat, a mood, a refrain, neglecting finer points such as the song's narrative arc and lyrical density. A similarly distracted attention prompts the listener to reject Eminem's prolific and varied output on the grounds of its insistent – occasionally extreme – profanity and sexual suggestiveness; these admittedly alienating and polarizing elements are both salient and integral to Eminem's themes, as they are to reality rap and gangsta rap in general,[4] but I would maintain that it is a distracted listener who chooses to dismiss the rapper's work on these grounds. If nothing else, the scale of Eminem's success should at least incite reflection on the cultural penetration and consumption of inflammatory speech.[5]

[3] Deleuze and Guattari theorize affect as independent of the organic bodies which produce and consume it; it is non-subjective, non-human and impervious to the passage of time. The creation of affects is proper to works of art (154-188).

[4] Adam Krims provides a useful typology of rap in his *Rap Music and the Politics of Identity*. Gangsta is a lucrative branch of reality rap, but the latter is broader in scope, undertaking to explore all facets of inner-city life (46-92).

[5] Eminem was the best-selling US artist of the noughties and his world-wide album sales to date are estimated at the 100 million mark (cf. "Eminem Discography").

A second species of mishearing consists in the cynical rebuttal of the professed 'authenticity' of the rapper's tale. Detractors argue that what we hear and see in a finished song and video is an elaborately recorded studio version of what remains, in the last instance, an unverifiable history, increasingly tailored to listener expectations. One of rap's major preoccupations, from the outset, has been to 'keep it real': to forge a narrative that keeps faith with ghetto life and the experience of the street, while refusing to sell out to a (predominantly white-owned, multinational) music industry. Leaving to one side, for the present, the distorting influence of the profit motive, it would be tempting to respond that objections levelled at the 'degree of reality' contained in a rap narrative are unanswerable and therefore unproductive – a blind alley. Philosophers have argued that fiction, in the active and positive sense of 'making' (fiction as derived from the Latin *fingere*, to shape or invent) is a condition of the narratability of experience as such and thus necessarily informs the 'real' as understood and later recounted: "The real", writes Jacques Rancière, "must be fictioned [*sic*] in order to be thought" (*Le partage du sensible* 61; my translation).[6] Rancière deliberately uses a neologism here – the coined French verb *fictionner* suggests, not so much a reworking, more a formatting of experience as the minimal precondition for intelligibility. In order to emerge as narratable object, the ghetto must be "fictioned". Its stories are narrated by a persona (the transgressive gangsta, the braggart, the sleazy pimp, the hedonistic, big-spending party animal, the victim turned avenging angel) who has his own perspective on the 'real'. We might add that the rapper's 'real' is 'signified', not told straight; the African American oral tradition of 'signifyin(g)', taken up by rap, implies heavy use of verbal play and deployment of a full armoury of rhetorical effects.[7] Charges of inauthenticity become more pertinent when one considers the artistic implications of gangsta rap's flagrant connivence with commerce; however, taken as aesthetic object *per se* – verse uttered to a powerful beat, punctuated by melodic hook and chorus – its hold on the 'real' is inevitably mediated and charges of inauthenticity, on this level at least, are neutralized. Imani Perry has this to say about the realism of rap: "[The 'real'] demands that artists maintain or use symbols asserting their allegiance to black youth populations [...]. It does not disallow fiction, imaginative constructions, or hip hop's traditional journey into myth" (87). The 'reality effect' of Eminem's song "Rock Bottom" derives as much from its raw depiction of a desperate young father on minimum wage, in and out of dead-end jobs, his daughter going barefoot and "down to her last diaper", as from the mythical evocation of an evil – heralded by the anticipatory slither of "spineless snakes" in the first verse – an evil that inspires covetousness and lust, the narrator turning criminal before our very eyes as he contemplates a Faustian pact: his soul in exchange for money, women and fame. The bending of rhymes throughout, especially in the final verse ("on 'em/flaunt 'em/pawn 'em/want 'em") mimics the elasticity of the narrator's morals as he yields to villainy. We last see him on "someone's lawn with guns drawn", the demure neatness of suburbia providing a darkly comic foil for the armed thief, his ammunition presumably primed for slaughter. It is this humour that both offsets the menacing tenor of the previous lines and heightens the pathos of the tale, lending it a

[6] The original reads: "Le réel doit être fictionné pour être pensé."

[7] On the history and aesthetics of 'signifyin(g)' cf. Henry Louis Gates, Jr. as well as Russell A. Potter (25-36).

degree of 'reality' that a mere litany of grievance – or tone of sustained *gravitas* – might fail to achieve.[8]

We come now to a third, and probably major reason why Eminem's narratives tend to go unheard – denunciation on grounds of gross political insensitivity. I refer to the moral panics generated by Eminem's profanity, by his unsparingly violent depictions of women in general and former wife in particular, his irreverence towards the machinery of state power, specifically George W. Bush (the MOSH video of 2004),[9] and the persistently homophobic strain which has earned him the displeasure of the Gay and Lesbian Alliance Against Defamation.[10] Any discussion of Eminem must deal squarely with the question of profanity, the enraged curses, the crude sexual taunts, the homophobic and misogynous slurs ('fag', 'lez', 'bitch') that hystericize the listener and consign the writing to a precarious life at the margins of the audible. While the temptations of contagious rage and condemnation are never distant, the interpellative force of Eminem's heated vocabulary must be resisted if we are to grasp anything of its broader social import. In her essay on the workings of linguistic harm, "Bad Words", Riley warns against the peculiar force of distraction exercised by offensive language:

> Bad words' peculiarly seductive distraction incites me to slip towards self-scrutiny, because another's angry interpellation so readily slides into becoming my own self-interpellation, where a thousand inducements to self-description, self-subjectification and self-diagnosis are anyway waiting eagerly at its service. (58)

To engage fully with Eminem's angry narratives of precarious life is to resist the distraction of identifying with injurious forms of address, to resist the "thousand inducements" to hyper-emotivity in the face of linguistic violence. Denunciation is an especially poor response to the cultural phenomenon of hateful speech, for reasons outlined by Judith Butler in the opening essay of her collection; while it may provide instant gratification and dissociation from guilt, denunciation also precludes responsibility, which Butler defines as the necessary act of "taking stock of our world" ("Explanation and Exoneration" 16-17). Outright rejection, like its obverse, unconditional worship, are hystericized responses which remain mired in what Lacan refers to as the 'imaginary' realm of the specular, with its primal, narcissistic love/hate oscillations; and Eminem does indeed inspire adulation from followers fixated on the cyclical rise and fall of their idol, prodigal in their expenditure of affect. The cult of celebrity and the voyeuristic appeal of misery appear, here, in their most naked form. An uncritically devoted fan-base that cathects Eminem's pain or qualifies his music with all-purpose superlatives must, however, remain blind to the culturally symbolic dimension of the rapper's variations on The Dark Side.

To the extremes of denunciation and worship must be added a further (mis)hearing of the Eminem misery narrative, which, I would suggest, dominates academic circuits of reception. Eminem's raps are judged too visible, too audible, too sensational, too self-

[8] Complete lyrics to Eminem's songs may be accessed at rapgenius.com. It is one of the more reliable sources and includes annotation (of varying quality) by hip hop heads and fans.

[9] This may be viewed at *youtube* (cf. "Mosh by Eminem" 2009).

[10] Cf. Nick Hasted (110-111; 122-124).

publicizing, too successful and therefore simply too complicit with the rampantly commodifying *ethos* of the mass music industry to maintain credibility as a record of ghetto experience, or command serious attention as aesthetically interesting pieces in their own right. Slick production values, brand naming and flaunting, the garishly busy circus of consumer culture, blatant sexual stereotype are not absent from Eminem's lyrics and videos, heightening the sense that the 'real' of reality rap has degenerated into caricature, or the crudely constructed 'real' of the TV reality show. But if we are prepared, with Fredric Jameson, to concede that "aesthetic production today has become integrated into commodity production generally" (4), that the commercialization of cultural forms is one of the defining traits of postmodernity, then the themes and visuals of rap might yet be usefully salvaged for the task of cultural criticism. To seek out hitherto uncommodified or uncommodifiable forms as the only legitimate objects of such criticism is to restrict one's efforts to a meagre and ever-shrinking terrain. Tricia Rose observes that "[h]ip hop has always been articulated via commodities and engaged in the revision of meanings attached to them" (*Black Noise* 41). Rap has a heavy stake in commodities; it could scarcely be otherwise, given the moment of its emergence. But its ironically self-conscious stance implies that it can play a part in revising, if not contesting, their meanings – or at least force a jaded public consciousness into acknowledgment of their dominion. At its best, rap forges a creative space out of its positioning as mass-consumed product; it makes poetry out of the forces that package and promote it; while this posture may not be one of resistance, neither is it one of unthinking acquiescence.

3. Conjuncture

A sense of the unprecedented interpenetration of the economic and aesthetic in what Jameson, after Mandel, has called the era of late capitalism leads to an alternative reading of the rap phenomenon that is Eminem. It is my contention that Eminem's narratives cannot be heard unless their idiom and form are fully contextualized, correlated to the moment of their production, and more specifically, to their linguistic conjuncture, a notion I intend to explore in what follows. This contextualization involves a salutary process of depersonalization, as we move from Eminem's private history – and demons – to Eminem as stylist, working out of a musical and lyrical tradition, while also responding fully to his cultural moment. It involves defetishization, as we cease to focus on Eminem's particularity – the victimized white boy having to prove himself in a black American musical form – and hear him as a virtuoso practitioner of the African American vernacular, which he renews and bends imaginatively to his own purposes. Eminem is a tribe unto himself. His avatars, Slim Shady and Marshall Mathers, his musical influences – IceT, the Beastie Boys, Rakim, Nas, Tupac Shakur – inspire a lyrical production that is arresting in its polyphony, its rootedness in a community of speech and topic. His stories of conflict, revenge and survival are entirely consistent with a genre whose recent ancestry lies in the ritualized street confrontations diversely known as 'signifyin(g)', 'sounding', and 'playing the dozens' (cf. Labov "Rules for Ritual Insults"). The paranoid swagger and self-aggrandizement, the adversarial stance and naked one-upmanship are generic requirements, amplified by rap's sonic force, its imagery and cultural penetration.

A fair – that is to say, responsible – hearing of Eminem's narratives requires consideration of the origins and effects of hate speech as it operates within a linguistic conjuncture, one that is currently witnessing a boom in the production and circulation of inflammatory scripts. I borrow the notion of linguistic conjuncture from Jean-Jacques Lecercle, who introduces it in his book *The Violence of Language*. Importing Althusser's concept of conjuncture into linguistics, Lecercle uses it to synthesize and supplant those of synchrony and diachrony. For Althusser, conjuncture is another name for the "backwardnesses, forwardnesses, survivals and unevennesses of development which *co-exist* in the structure of the real historical present" (qtd. in *Violence of Language* 205). In a similar vein, Raymond Williams speaks of the "residual", "dominant" and "emergent" forms and trends perceptible at a given historical moment (121-127). For Lecercle, language is the paradigmatic social formation; it is a repository of residual, dominant and emergent practices and forms, each of which generates effects of sense in the present, each of which is subject to specific rates of change. Discursive formations (the languages of literature, politics, economics, medicine etc.) evolve according to one time-scale, while each component of language as social practice (lexicon, dialect, syntax) evolves in relation to another. A linguistic conjuncture is both arbitrary and unstable: language change is non-teleological, while discursive formations are endlessly refashioned over time. The term 'conjuncture' captures the non-autonomy of language in its ceaseless and dynamic interaction with the social, economic and political to which it is inextricably bound or 'con-joined' (*Violence of Language* 201-205). It is precisely a sense of the *non*-autonomy of excitable speech – its *conjunction* with extra-linguistic factors – that is required if we are to gain some insight into its current visibility and social penetration.

What, then, are the dominant vocabularies inflecting our linguistic conjuncture? Why do profanity and the explicit lyric sell and fascinate as they do in our discursive *milieu*? How are they 'con-joined' to existing practices and norms? By way of response, we might consider the economic and political ideas shaping our moment and the major discursive formations that give these ideas substance. There are two interconnecting points I would wish to make here.

Firstly, Anglo-American globalizing neoliberalism and the new "spirit of capitalism" (Boltanski and Chiapello) have generated an impressive lexicon in a wide range of social practices and spheres. A great deal of painstaking work has been done on this topic by the school of Critical Discourse Analysis (CDA), spearheaded by Norman Fairclough.[11] English as global language is the prime vehicle and exporter of the neoliberal *doxa*: the ideology of communication, the sanitized codes of interpersonal address, the brittle market-driven vocabulary of consumer choice, rights and satisfaction, the workplace watchwords of flexibility, performance, and quality control. Vincent B. Leitch has suggested that a "market-oriented perspective conditions not only our thoughts and decisions, but our imaginations and futures" (107) and political philosopher Michael Sandel charts our passage from "*having* a market economy to *being* a market society" (10). In its role as primary vehicle of social engineering and exchange,

[11] For a synthetic and representative work, cf. Fairclough.

language both serves and preserves this hegemonic, market-oriented order. In the concluding section of his book, *Une philosophie marxiste du langage* (197-206), Lecercle identifies a number of features that might constitute a spontaneous neoliberal philosophy of language: an emphasis on language as instrument of cooperative communication; the *langue de coton*, or language of limp consensus, embodied in the virtually indistinguishable rallying cries coming from 'left' and 'right' of the political spectrum; and 'spin', a linguistic technique designed to enhance governmental messages and steer public opinion and political debate toward predefined ends. Alongside these sanitized practices and upbeat vocabularies there lie the realities of neoliberal economic policy as experienced by millions around the world. Here, the rift between rhetoric and reality cannot fail to strike the imagination. David Harvey provides a particularly cogent account of the human and environmental cost of globalizing the neoliberal model in his *Brief History of Neoliberalism* (cf. esp. 152-182): the creation of a 'flexible' workforce which in effect becomes a disposable one; a trashed environment, commodified for profit; the racialization and feminization of poverty; the feminization of degrading labour; massive populations living at or below subsistence levels; powers of organized labour weakened, by-passed, or violently destroyed. Etienne Balibar has characterized the effects of neoliberal policy as a form of "ultra-objective violence" or "cruelty without a face" (143). On the one hand, the dominant, limply consensual, cosily inclusive, aspirational, market-inspired discourses of our time, fuelling the reiterated murmur of the *doxa*; on the other, the effects of objective violence – that of 'actually existing' neoliberalism – on populations both near and far afield. The breach between the two cannot fail to generate affect, an affect that is at pains to find politically constructive outlets and a language that matches its intensity.[12] It could be argued that incendiary lyrics afford it a measure of release. We must imagine a capture, an arrest of language by affect. It is worth remembering that rap emerged in an urban context (mid-70s New York) where euphemistic vocabularies of 'urban renewal', 'economic restructuring', 'slum clearance' and 'relocation' translated as a systematic assault on the poorest sectors of the population – black and Hispanic working-class communities were uprooted, destroyed and further fragilized by employment loss due to rapid processes of deindustrialization. Eminem's formative environment – 80s Detroit – was riven by similar tensions, with its impoverished black inner-city ghettos, its 'white flight' suburbs with their lines of demarcation between areas of affluence and 'trailer-trash' poverty. In such conjunctures, one cannot account for the insistent performance of offensive speech, its citation, its circulation, its bankability simply by claiming that it is generic, a lurid gangsta idiom which happens to appeal to white suburban teenagers; it cannot be explained away by invoking, *pace* Wordsworth, a "spontaneous overflow of powerful feelings" – a high-octane verbal performance as therapeutic venting of private past wrongs. Nor is it to be put down to the battle codes of ritualized insult, although these factors have their part to play. Incendiary language provides its speaker with a "script of rage" (Riley 53); its hold on the imagination derives only partly from the voyeuristic allure of commodified violence. It is, crucially, conditioned by linguistic conjuncture. The 'bad words' of Eminem's narratives capture and disseminate an affect that testifies to the inadequacy of available languages of resistance. This affect cannot be detached from the historical

[12] Here and in what follows I am indebted to the analysis of Peter Sloterdijk (183-229).

moment that bears witness (in horror, exaltation or indifference) to its birth; enlisting their vitriol in the service of his story, the rapper is also interpellated or 'captured' by these words as potent carriers of a dispersed or homeless rage, the signature affect of his times.[13]

Secondly, we must consider the discursive properties of the 'post-political' moment, as it is known to its detractors. Chantal Mouffe has argued that our conflict-averse, supposedly consensual times negate antagonism, which she understands as the very motor of political life. When the sense of a political adversary disappears – as, for instance, after the collapse of the Soviet Union – the stage is set for politics to slip into what Mouffe calls "the moral register" (5); political antagonisms are reformulated in terms of 'right' and 'wrong', 'good' and 'evil' (cf. Mouffe 72-76). We no longer engage in heated polemics with an adversary; we plot and scheme to eradicate a sworn enemy. US political rhetoric, from Ronald Reagan's 'Evil Empire' to George W. Bush's 'Axis of Evil' strikes one in this connection, as does the ill-fated 'Operation Infinite Justice' thought up by Pentagon officials in 2001 as a name for the US military response to the 9/11 attacks. For Mouffe, the moralization of political discourse signals the end of vibrantly democratic, agonistic debate, and announces the era of uncontested neoliberal hegemony, which secretes its own sporadic, unpredictable forms of violence but offers no reasoned alternative to the *status quo*. Similarly preoccupied with the present conjuncture, Rancière traces the moralizing tenor of political discourse to a recent shift in the collective understanding of the traumatic events that have shaped the 20th century – Soviet crimes, the Shoah. These, he asserts, have become paradigmatic examples of absolute Evil, an Evil divorced from the monstrous actions of specific regimes, an Evil exceeding "all juridical and political measure" (*Dissensus* 103). The philosopher explicitly correlates this quasi-ethical apprehension of the event and its inflated rhetoric to an eclipse of the political – a case of ethics displacing politics. The shift into the "moral register", the depoliticization of historical events, the readiness of politicians to demonize their adversaries rather than polemicize with them set the discursive tone of the 'post-political' moment. Emergent cultural forms cannot be unaffected by these developments. The comic-strip, 'horror-core' evil affected by Eminem and his earlier avatars, Slim Shady and Marshall Mathers, is an inverted, ironic image of the self-styled, self-appointed 'good' US as global peacekeeper. The affect-soaked lyrics and body language, the aggression levelled at 'haters', the undying devotion sworn to mentors and fans alike mimics, in the mode of parodic hyperbole, the narrowed, manichean friend/foe imaginary of much contemporary political rhetoric.

Cultural forms are conjoined to political and economic mutations and their discursive enactments. The content, tone, language and delivery of Eminem's rap narratives resonates with these determinant forces and gives life to their contradictions. The reception of his songs becomes a precarious affair. Banished, to all intents and purposes, from a consensual political field, antagonism resurfaces in brute and primal form as the creative motor of rap, at least in its gangsta and reality modes. *Agon* is its driving force.

[13] Cf. Peter Sloterdijk on the "political homelessness of rage" in postcommunist times (214). Eminem's visibility tends to occlude the fact that his language is that of a *milieu*, a collectivity; the gangsta sociolect is practised with verve by Dr Dre, Lil' Wayne, 50 Cent, to name only a(n) (in)famous few.

This generic pugnacity meshes with the competitive and individualistic drives unleashed and promoted by a market-centred ideology to amplify the narrative in ways that the listener finds simultaneously riveting and repellent. Swagger and bragging, naked ambition and the uninhibited pursuit of wealth, the visual and verbal referencing of brand and commodity are not absent from Eminem's stories of precarious life. These motifs may well be rooted in traditional rap forms – braggadocio, the ego trip – but they are also entirely consistent with the *ethos* of Sandel's "market society", and if the listener recoils from them, she does so with a shock of recognition. The mechanism that comes to her rescue here is that of denial, buttressed by the contagious anger provoked by inflammatory lyrics. Recognition gives way to indignation, alienation, denunciation and all possibility of hearing is foreclosed. Eminem's narratives of precarious life unfold on a knife-edge. The forces of commodification exercised by the music industry promote forms of distracted attention, steering the listener away from conjuncture, towards the song as finite and consumable unit, accompanied by elaborate visuals, animated by the sophisticated interplay of rhymed lyrics and beat, with sex and profanity providing an added *frisson*. The repeated performance of rage harbours its own perils; self-parody, affect-fatigue, the monotony of the *déjà vu*. Incendiary speech threatens, at every step, to overwhelm lyrical content and technical virtuosity. In this day and age, affects are consumable quantities, and there is no doubt that Eminem's narratives successfully trade in (and on) pain, fury, vengefulness and spite. Yet these precarious records of precarious life are, at their best, the unlikely, pitch-perfect poetry of our time; a scabrous poetry functioning as a provisional "rage collection point" (Sloterdijk 183) – perhaps one of the more fully-realized aesthetic expressions of what one might imagine as the neoliberal unconscious.

Works Cited

Balibar, Etienne. "Violence, Ideality and Cruelty." *Politics and the Other Scene*. 2002. By Etienne Balibar. Trans. Christine Jones, James Swenson, and Chris Turner. London and New York: Verso, 2011. 129-145.

Benjamin, Walter. "The Work of Art in the Age of Mechanical Reproduction." 1936. *Illuminations: Essays and Reflections*. By Walter Benjamin. Ed. Hannah Arendt. Trans. Harry Zohn. London: Fontana Press, 1992. 211-244.

Boltanski, Luc, and Eve Chiapello. *The New Spirit of Capitalism*. Trans. Gregory Elliott. New York and London: Verso, 2007.

Butler, Judith. "Explanation and Exoneration, or What We Can Hear." *Precarious Life: The Powers of Mourning and Violence*. By Judith Butler. London and New York: Verso, 2004. 1-18.

—. "Precarious Life." *Precarious Life: The Powers of Mourning and Violence*. By Judith Butler. London and New York: Verso, 2004. 128-151.

Deleuze, Gilles, and Félix Guattari. *Qu'est-ce que la philosophie?*. 1991. Paris: Les Éditions de Minuit, 2005.

8-mile. Dir. Curtis Hanson. Perf. Eminem, Kim Basinger, and Brittany Murphy. Universal Pictures, 2002. DVD

Eminem. "Sing for the Moment." *The Eminem Show*. Shady Records, 2002.

—. "Rock Bottom." *The Slim Shady LP*. Aftermath and Interscope Records, 1999.

—. "The Way I Am." *Marshall Mathers*. Aftermath and Interscope Records, 2000.

"Eminem Discography." *Wikipedia*. 2013. Retrieved 4 Oct. 2013. <http://en.wikipedia.org/wiki/Eminem_discography>.

Gates, Henry Louis, Jr. *The Signifying Monkey: A Theory of Afro-American Literary Criticism*. Oxford: Oxford University Press, 1988.

Harvey, David. *A Brief History of Neoliberalism*. Oxford: Oxford University Press, 2005.

Hasted, Nick. *The Dark Story of Eminem*. 2003. London and New York: Omnibus, 2011.

Jameson, Fredric. *Postmodernism, or, the Cultural Logic of Late Capitalism*.1991. London and New York: Verso, 1995.

Krims, Adam. *Rap Music and the Politics of Identity*. Cambridge: Cambridge University Press, 2001.

Labov, William. "Rules for Ritual Insults." *Language in the Inner City: Studies in the Black English Vernacular*.1972. Oxford: Blackwell, 1977. 297-353.

Lecercle, Jean-Jacques. *The Violence of Language*. London and New York: Routledge, 1990.

—. *Une philosophie marxiste du langage*. Paris: PUF, 2004.

Leitch, Vincent B. *Theory Matters*. London and New York: Routledge, 2003.

"Mosh by Eminem: Interscope." Online video clip. InterscopeGeffenAM. *Youtube*. 15 June 2009. Retrieved 9 Dec. 2013. http://www.youtube.com/watch?v=Ox0Q4YIdnGI>.

Mouffe, Chantal. *On the Political*. Oxford and New York: Routledge, 2005.

Perry, Imani. *Prophets of the Hood: Politics and Poetics in Hip Hop*. Durham, NC: Duke University Press, 2004.

Potter, Russell A. *Spectacular Vernaculars: Hip-Hop and the Politics of Postmodernism*. Albany: State University of New York Press, 1995.

Rancière, Jacques. *Le partage du sensible: Esthétique et politique*. Paris: La Fabrique, 2000.

—. *Dissensus: On Politics and Aesthetics*. Trans. Steven Corcoran. London & New York: Continuum, 2010.

Riley, Denise. "Bad Words." *The Force of Language*. By Jean-Jacques Lecercle and Denise Riley. Basingstoke and New York: Macmillan, 2004. 46-62.

Rose, Tricia. *Black Noise: Rap Music and Black Culture in Contemporary America*. Hanover, NH: Wesleyan University Press, 1994.

—. *The Hip Hop Wars: What We Talk About When We Talk About Hip Hop – and Why It Matters*. New York: Basic Books, 2008.

Sandel, Michael. *What Money Can't Buy: The Moral Limits of Markets*. 2012. London and New York: Penguin, 2013.

Sloterdijk, Peter. *Rage and Time*: A *Psychopolitical Investigation*. 2006. Trans. Mario Wenning. New York: Columbia University Press, 2010.

Spivak, Gayatri Chakravorty. "Can the Subaltern Speak?". *Marxism and the Interpretation of Culture*. Ed. Cary Nelson and Lawrence Grossberg. Urbana and Chicago: University of Illinois Press, 1988. 271-313.

Williams, Raymond. *Marxism and Literature*. Oxford: Oxford University Press, 1977.

Marc Amfreville

Vulnerability, Literature and Ethics in Sapphire's *Push*

Judith Butler's book *Precarious Life* was subtitled *The Powers of Mourning and Violence*. Although it dealt specifically with the aftermath of 9/11 at the national and global levels, the words mourning and violence might well have been used to describe the highly individualized – intimate to the point sometimes of obscenity – contents of Sapphire's 1996 *Push*. This stunning novel, in the form of the main character's contribution to her alternative-school journal, is the fictitious first-person account of a victim of outright violence, and constitutes in the Freudian sense a work of mourning.

As the novel opens, Precious – the heroine's bitterly paradoxical middle name – is pregnant for the second time with her father's baby: "I was left back when I was twelve because I had a baby for my fahver. That was in 1983. This gonna be my scond baby" (Sapphire 3). This is actually the opening sentence of the novel and it deals a triple blow to the reader, who is hit by the revelation of a sixteen-year old having had two babies already, and by the seemingly quiet suggestion of an incest. Precious's first child – a four-year old girl with Down's syndrome – is raised by her grandmother but is smuggled back into the house for social services visits and goes on justifying welfare checks paid to Precious's mother. As the chronologically shuffled text moves on, we also learn that Precious has been raped by both her parents from the earliest age, that she has been constantly battered by her mother to the point of giving birth to her first child on the kitchen floor – which caused the poorly oxygenated newborn baby permanent brain damage on top of her genetic malformation and incestuous heredity –, and finally that her father contaminated her with the HIV virus.

Within this horrendously realistic framework, the story which is told is also that of a school journal, probably written after the main events took place, since the experience described in the narrative present is concerned with the young girl's acquisition of reading and writing skills, which are totally non-existent at the outset of chapter 1 when Precious, aged sixteen, is kicked out of regular school because of her second pregnancy. In other words, the text, aside from being a naturalistic plunge into contemporary Harlem – the reader gradually comes to the conclusion that Abdul, the second child, was born in 1988 –, lends itself to being read not as the result of a healing process, but as the healing process itself, the work of mourning which eventually enables Precious to overcome trauma, become herself and live her own life – in the time left to her by Aids.

Such a novel, based on the writer's seven-year experience as a teacher and social worker in Harlem, may obviously help us deal with the question of vulnerability, by which I mean the question of a human being's susceptibility to injury. In many respects though, no character could be more foreign to an academic collection of essays than obese, illiterate, misery-ridden, insanity-threatened Precious. But I want to argue that the importance of Sapphire's novel lies elsewhere, as she manages to provoke for her protagonist not sympathy in the usual compassionate, often voyeuristic and ultimately comfortable sense, but to create an inescapable sense of 'fellowship'. In order to support this argument, I propose to call upon three concepts borrowed from the Freudian clinic of trauma and more precisely from his 1895 little-read essay, "Project for a Scientific Psychology": *Bahnung* (facilitation), *Nebenmensch* (the fellow being) and *Hilflosigkeit* (helplessness). It is a very early text, which deals mainly with the neuronal system from a physiological point of view, but it also contains elements that Freud would later develop.

1. *Bahnung*

While the original German word *Bahnung* is more graphically vivid in terms of its almost geographical, geological even, sense (and while the French *frayage* remains quite obscure to many readers), the English 'facilitation' alludes to the consequence rather than to the occurrence of the first usually irretrievable trauma. *Bahnung* refers to the repeated passage of excitation along the same pathway, one that brings about a gradual and permanent decrease in resistance to its progression. Taken from the other end of the time line, that is to say the present narration of a trauma victim, the reader or the therapist almost always first encounters evidence of a second trauma, an unmanageable influx of excitation caused by pain, fear, astonishment, which in many ways serves to hide from consciousness the contents of a preceding breakthrough. It often happens that this first trauma reveals itself to be in fact second or third in line, the wound left in the psyche having thus 'facilitated' the later occurrences.[1] Brought to bear on our text, and to the functioning of incestuous rape in general, Freud's concept proves particularly effective. Let us read again the opening lines:

> I was left back when I was twelve because I had a baby for my fahver. That was 1983. I was out of school for a year. *This* gonna be my second baby. My daughter got Down Sinder. She's retarded. I had got left back in the second grade too, when I was seven, 'cause I couldn't read (and still peed on myself). (3; italics mine)

Precious's latest trauma is easily identifiable: she is pregnant with her father's child at sixteen ("This" referring to the textual present). There is also the presence of an earlier shock: Precious had her first baby by the same genitor five years earlier. Then comes the indication of clear signs of an even anterior trauma, as the learning process is hindered and sphincter-control failings occur at moments of unbearable stress. The gradual recapturing of events – favoured by the writing process, and to a lesser extent in the case of Precious, by the counselling sessions – will successively give us access to repeated raping by her father from the age of seven (an experience she had not forgotten), to deeply buried traumatic traces of sexual predation by her mother, and the ultimate revelation by her mother's guiltless confession that the child had first been

[1] For further developments, cf. Amfreville, particularly chapter 1, which summarizes major theoretical insights on trauma, most notably Freud's and Ferenczi's.

abused and raped while still in her diapers. What Sapphire's fiction strikingly captures – this is indeed true to real-life cases – is that not all traumatic memories are repressed and disappear from waking consciousness. Some indeed do, as the mother's repeated raping, while others are remembered but fail to be organized in the form of a narrative. They surge back to awareness as unrelated flashes, or nightmares, very much in the way soldiers' traumas operate. The very functioning of the book thus imitates, is a mimesis of, a repeatedly injured brain.

A word has to be added about another feature of this properly 'extra-ordinary' book. As ghastly as its contents may sound, the tone remains so totally exempt of self-pity, the narration so much away from any easy sensational effect, that the reader does shudder but never recoils. What has to be made clear then, leaving aside the gripping dimension of such exposed suffering, is the way this narrative, in spite of its apparent illiteracy and disorganization, obeys the extremely codified functioning of an incest-traumatized psyche. It may be worth noting here that the writer, although stemming from a bourgeois background, was also the victim of incest as a child.

Precious's intelligence is impaired, her learning abilities hindered, and her body has transformed itself into an ugly mass. This was undoubtedly meant to protect her from her father's lust, but the change resulted in accrued vulnerability, the man being obviously drawn to her 'shapes' and Precious being subjected at a very early age to her schoolfellows' paralysing taunting. To this terribly candid presentation, one must add the most harrowing admission that Precious cannot help deriving physical pleasure – orgasms even – from intercourse with her father. She may therefore be said to develop *borderline* behaviours with clearly schizoid components – although never referred to as such. Precious is indeed the victim of spaced out moments, in which she is prey to PTSD, or hallucinations, in which both her parents assault her in turns (13).

Sapphire's text evinces a truly clinical precision here, showing Precious as capable of questioning her delirium, that is of doubting the reality of her hallucination. She is thus 'borderline', not 'psychotic', as is exemplified by a passage like this: "Early on, I realize no one hear the TV set voices growing out blackboard but me so I try not to answer them" (38). Paratactic syntax at times recaptures the incomprehensible swirling of past and present, added to an incapacity to assimilate sexual contents: "My head water. I see bad things. I see my daddy. I see TVs I hear rap music I want something to eat I want fuck feeling from Daddy I want die I want die" (53). As she becomes more and more alienated, Push constantly opposes her real physical appearance – very dark, 5 foot 10, over 200 pounds – to the frail, light-skinned, straight-haired girl she believes she is 'inside'. More to the point even than this failure of narcissism – "I hate myself" is a leitmotiv –, time collapses for Precious, in a way rendered possible by the 'facilitation' at work in her psyche:

> I am twelve, no I was twelve, when that shit happen. I am 16 now. For past couple of weeks or so, ever since white bitch Lichenstein kick me outta school shit, 1983 and 1987, twelve years old and sixteen years old, first baby and this one coming, all been mixed up in my head. Mama jus' hit me wif fryin'pan? Baby, brand new and wrapped in white blankets, or fat and dead eyed lying in crib at my grandmother's house. Everything seems like clothes in washing machine at laundry mat – round 'n round, up'n down. One minute

> Mama's foot smashing into side of my head, next I'm jumping over desk on Mrs Lichenstein's ass. (21-22)

It should perhaps be recalled that such time confusion – masterfully exemplified in Benjy's famous monologue at the outset of Faulkner's *The Sound and the Fury* – is indeed characteristic of psychotic subjects who live in a sort of eternal present, or rather in a time in which past and present both collapse and exclude each other.[2]

As is very often the case in real life, repeated incest also results in a loss of bodily perception: "Why can't I see myself, feel where I end and begin?" (Sapphire 31). The direct consequence of this is self-inflicted pain and scarification – not as a masochistic pleasure-seeking gesture, but rather as a frantic search for evidence of one's corporeal limits, and ultimately of one's existence – alternating with death wishes: "My body not mine I hate it coming [...]. I bite my fingernails till they look like disease, pull strips of my skin away... [...] Cut cut cut arm wrist, not trying to die, trying to plug myself back in" (112). In the very logic of the text, that is Precious's vision of her own fate, there may have been no way out of a gradual dissolution of the self, had it not been for the watershed meeting with Blue Rain.

2. *Nebenmensch*

Also taken from Freud's "Project", the term *Nebenmensch* is not to be confused with *Nachbar*, one's neighbour, or with *Nächste*, one's fellow human being, understood in its Christian sense (constantly used in the Gospels). It refers rather to a being – who can be the mother but also somebody else - who helps the infant grow up by remaining next to him/her, and by functioning as his/her 'interlocutor'. The *Nebenmensch* is not therefore a mere agent of physical satisfaction for basic needs. As Monique Schneider has recently shown, the *Nebenmensch*, *l'être proche*, or 'fellow being', can also refer to 'a figure' during the child's development or even in adulthood who, by standing near the subject, provides a lateral (as opposed to a reflexive one) vision, such for example as that of Fliess 'near' Freud in the course of the advance of psychoanalytical theory.

Before we try to assess the relevance of this concept in the novel, it should perhaps be noted that Sapphire chose as her protagonist a teenager who has it in her to fight, and who believes in herself sufficiently not to drown completely in mental disease. For example, she knows that the IQ tests she takes are wrong: "There has always been something wrong with the tesses. The tesses paint a picture of me wif no brain. The tesses paint a picture of me an'my muver – my whole family, we more than dumb, we invisible" (30). We are very close here to the considerations developed by Marie Gaille and Sandra Laugier when they analyse vulnerability in terms of a closeness to the animal "dumb" condition. There are yet clear literary allusions in Precious's diatribe, notably to Ralph Ellison's *Invisible Man*. Langston Hughes, Toni Morrison, or Alice Walker are also present, and Monica Michlin has brilliantly analyzed these references and shown how they pay homage to such famous Black figures, but also take their distance from a reading that Sapphire undoubtedly considers as sometimes too narrowly

[2] For further developments on that point, cf. Abensour (particularly chapter 3, 71-91).

communitarian.[3] The book is dedicated to "children everywhere", and a quote from Blake's "Tyger" in Precious's diary (128) makes sure the text is read as a passage from a tale of innocence to a song of experience.

This is where the importance of the *Nebenmensch* figure makes itself manifest. As the title clearly indicates – "Push" being a reference both to the moment of child delivery and to the teacher's encouragement to force words out of her student's brain and give them materiality on paper – there is a sense of rebellion left in Precious, and she still feels the pain which is the first condition for healing: "I been out of the picture so long I am used to it. But that don't mean it don't hurt" (32). Psychotic numbing or fragmentation would be alternative 'solutions' for the psyche to deal with injury, as is explained by Ferenczi, but the subject would then be much less accessible to therapeutic help, such as the remedial teacher – Precious's 'fellow being' – is made to represent in the novel. Precious definitely owes her psychic salvation to Blue Rain, a teacher whose name subtly alludes to Sapphire's and who starts off by giving her a sense of belonging. Hers is what I would call an ethical approach of vulnerability.

This is how Precious's first day at the alternative school starts: "Is I Miz Rain, I axes, is I in the right place? She hand me tissue, say: Yes, Precious, yes" (48). It is most striking to see how the teenager's assumed name thus suddenly acquires the value of a term of endearment. Only then can real remedial work begin. Blue Rain's method should be described carefully, her role being quite clearly that suggested by Freud's concept of *Nebenmensch*. The students who cannot read or write beyond the alphabet and very vague phonetic transcriptions are told to transcribe what is on their minds: "Push yourself to see the letters that represent the words you're thinking […]. Precious what's on your mind?... […] What you was thinking just then? I go to open my mouth. She say: Don't say it, *write* it" (61). After a second of understandable hesitation, Precious writes: "li Mg o mi m" (61). Then the teacher asks Precious to read what she wrote: "I reads: Little Mongo on my mind" (61). Blue Rain then writes the sentence underneath, followed by a written question: "Who is Little Mongo?" (61); and Precious is made to write the answer. Our understanding of the method starts when we read: "I copy Little Mongo's name from where Miz Rain had wrote it" (61). What we are dealing with here is obviously this ideal mixture of proximity and distance which Freud implicitly defines as ideally informing the relationship with the 'fellow being'. There is proximity because Blue Rain comes as close to Precious's emotion as the latter will allow, but there is also distance as the teacher never substitutes her own words for her pupil's. She respectfully transcribes what she is given to read and thus allows her student to gradually appropriate written language. We shall not go into further detail since the account is in itself remarkably terse, but we should pause to underscore the emotional bonding entailed by this ethical acceptance of vulnerability.

Precious paradoxically starts feeling lonely. In other words, she starts having access to her own feelings of deprivation. Care and love have been replaced by violence and sexual predation to such a traumatic extent that emotional response had disappeared but is now made possible again. As a ferrywoman, Sapphire takes Precious across the Hades river of pain, she becomes the necessary mediator between Precious, the physical

[3] I wish to thank Monica Michlin for sharing her essay and her enthusiasm for Sapphire's novel with me.

person who is learning to read, and Precious, the traumatized psyche, invaded by memory flashes, surges of violence and self-destroying drives: "I say I drownin' in river. She don't lookt me like I'm crazy but sayn if you just sit there the river gonna rise up drown you. Writing could be the boat carry you to the other side.... Open your notebook, Precious... you gotta push. And I do" (97) Having gained access to her own helplessness, broken through the mass of flesh and inertia she had built around herself, Precious starts naming prior actions. The story of the father's sexual behaviour has been established by the reader long before Precious comes up with the utterance "I think I was rape", which occurs only on page 69. Through the mediation of writing, the girl realizes that she never wanted what happened – while the physical pleasure she took seemed to indicate the opposite in her guilt-ridden mind. There is now room for clearly directed anger: "Nigger rape me. I not steal shit fat bitch your husband RAPE me RAPE ME!" (74). She is now capable of acting against her mother – by having her almost unwittingly cut off welfare, or by running away from her house for ever – because she realizes she had not received protection from her. "I am alive inside. Mama and Daddy is not win. I'm winning" (131).

Fortunately for the book's literary value – our sophisticated academic type of reading tends to minimize the value of exaggeratedly optimistic endings –, Precious has been infected with Aids. Aside from the sociological verisimilitude, probably grounded on the writer's field experience, such a proleptic ending has a symbolic value: suddenly the name "Precious" seems to have lost all its bitter irony. Sapphire's novel is not about magical redemption and salvation; the root of evil metaphorically remains inside the young woman's body as a promise of death, but mediation will have helped her make the most of her own story. What also counts symbolically is that Precious's child is *not* contaminated by HIV: there is therefore a possible future.

3. *Hilflosigkeit*

In order to fully measure the implications of such an ethical approach of vulnerability, I propose to make a final detour through Freud's third concept, which will help me reach a conclusion. *Hilflosigkeit* means helplessness. Here the utter helplessness of the girl-child is represented by Precious being raped before the age of two, while sharing a bed with both her parents. As in the case of the Aids infection, this horrendously realistic scene (in its implications more than in its actual wording) does not preclude a symbolical relevance. While there is a synecdochal value attached to such a depiction of an Afro-American Harlem family as the emblem of a totally deprived fringe of the population, the representation of the helplessness that is involved demands a response that should be *both* emotional and ethical.

In a lecture entitled "Precarious Life, the Obligation of Proximity", Judith Butler starts by drawing from Levinas: it is the otherness that acts upon us in such accounts; we are, to borrow her words, "affronted by something from the outside", and while "receptivity is one of the conditions of action", utter empathy – i.e., the confusion between the subject's condition and our own – would be ethically unacceptable. What Butler wishes to promote instead is the "reversibility of proximity and distance", which I take to mean something akin to what the character of Blue Rain achieves in the novel, i.e., a *constantly renewed* process of reduction and extension of the interval between the "precarious subject" and the witness of the patient's plight, be it the teacher or the reader: "A good reader is like a detective, she say, looking for clues in the text. A good reader is like you Precious, she say. Passionate! Passionately involved with whut they are reading" (Sapphire 108). One cannot help thinking here of Poe's poet/mathematician detective, Dupin: in order to unearth meaning, Dupin both identifies with the subject of his investigation *and* remains at a respectful distance, so that he manages to bring his emotions into play and use them as clues.[4] The same could be said of the psychoanalyst's ideally distanced study of his/her counter-transference, which cannot take place if he/she does not first let him/herself be vulnerably shot through by her/his patient's experience. The same could also be said of Sapphire's position: did she not use her most intimate experience of helplessness to gain access to her former students' precariousness; did she not also find the necessary distance by imagining an 'other' protagonist, thus casting herself simultaneously into the role of the victim *and* of the healer? The same might finally be said of us, professional critics. We are well aware of the need for an intellectual distance from our object of study. Perhaps too well aware. Would not our work gain in relevance if we grounded our attention in the awareness of our own vulnerability? After all, does not reading 'passionately' mean reading 'in pain'?

Works Cited

Abensour, Liliane. *La Tentation psychotique.* Paris: PUF, 2008.

Amfreville, Marc. *Ecrits en souffrance.* Paris: Michel Houdiard, 2009.

Butler, Judith. *Precarious Life. The Powers of Mourning and Violence.* 2004. New York: Verso Books, 2006.

—. "Precarious Life: the Obligations of Proximity." The Neale Wheeler Watson Lecture 2011. *Nobel Museum.* 8 June 2011. Retrieved 11 July 2013. <http://www.youtube.com/watch?v=BHBFxUSdJ7s>.

Freud, Sigmund. "Project for a Scientific Psychology." 1895. *The Complete Psychological Works of Sigmund Freud.* Vol. 1. London: The Hogarth Press, 1966. 295-397.

Laugier, Sandra (with Marie Gaille and Sylvie Servoise). *Grammaires de la vulnérabilité.* Paris: PUPS, 2011.

Michlin, Monica. "Narrative as Empowerment: *Push* and the Signifying on Prior African-American Novels in Incest." *Etudes Anglaises* 2 (April-June 2006): 169-185.

Sapphire. *Push.* 1996. New York: Vintage, 1997.

Schneider, Monique. *La Détresse aux sources de l'éthique.* Paris: Le Seuil, 2011.

[4] Cf. Poe's famous detective tales, "Murders in the Rue Morgue", "The Purloined Letter" and "The Mystery of Marie Roget".

Hélène Aji

A Survival Kit: The Poetics of Precariousness in Lyn Hejinian's "Happily"

> Constantly I write this happily
> Hazards that hope may break open my lips [...].
> (Hejinian, "Happily" 385)

The first lines of Lyn Hejinian's poem "Happily" remind us that, "constantly" and "happily", her poems struggle between determinacy and the anxiety of indeterminacy, between closure and "the rejection of closure" – to quote the title of her 1983 famous essay –, between ideology and the debunking of ideological discourse. By questioning the very form of expression in language, this major member of the American Language Poets group has been elaborating alternate modes of expression that eschew the sentimentality of self-expression. In "The Rejection of Closure", Hejinian unfolds the complexities and paradoxes of a poetics that seeks to reconcile the contradictory impulses of "boundedness" and "openness":

> Writing's initial situation, its point of origin, is often characterized and always complicated by opposing impulses in the writer and by a seeming dilemma that language creates and then cannot resolve. The writer experiences a conflict between a desire to satisfy a demand for boundedness, for containment and coherence, and a simultaneous desire for free, unhampered access to the world prompting a correspondingly open response to it. (41)

According to Hejinian, this dilemma of the writer is to be recontextualized in terms of the simultaneous definitions of her subjectivity and of her relationship to the world. In aesthetic terms, these definitions entail formal decisions which are, very often, double-edged. Clearly inscribed in the debate over the consequences of formalism, and of the deliberate choice of formal poetics over free verse made by the Language Poets, her argument counters the assertion according to which form implies closure, whereas the openness of the open work can only be conveyed through the dismissal of fixed forms. To return to the issues at hand with the notion of precariousness, form would mean the refusal of the idea of flux, unexpected changes and the general frailty of human bearings. It would then seem logical to come to the conclusion that for a text to be able to take into account reality's unpredictable turns, and human living's precarious and temporary moments of equilibrium, one would require the free and far-ranging compositional modes of Charles Olson and Robert Duncan's field composition, one based on association, improvisation and to some extent the open-ended generation of texts. The precarious text might in this respect be nothing but an unfinished text. However, the division and the contradiction is not so radical, and Lyn Hejinian suggests that formalism and "openness," or the capability to intregrate a reality in flux, can produce modes of reflecting the elusive desire for infinity, and the recognition of finitude:

> These areas of conflict are not neatly parallel. Form does not necessarily achieve closure, nor does raw materiality provide openness. Indeed, the conjunction of *form* with radical *openness* may be what can offer a version of the 'paradise' for which writing often yearns–a flowering focus on a distinct infinity. (42)

This is definitely the "paradise" Hejinian sought to create with "Happily". The poem was written following her recovery from cancer, and it underscores the poet's relief, the 'happiness' of survival, which, however, inexorably mingles with the sentiment of pointlessness, and sheer chance. 'Happiness' is therefore made to signify what happens in unfathomable ways, the process of living maybe, not the aim everyone pursues for itself. To be 'happy' is not to be equated with this feeling of elation or comfort we think it is; it coincides rather with this acceptance of a flow in which one is disoriented and adrift. 'Happiness' is then perceived as the fleeting and terrifying moment when the subject realizes her unpredictable ephemerality, and life is experienced as precariousness itself, with heightened moments of awareness when it is threatened, made palpably vulnerable. The poetic enterprise consequently turns into an obstinate, and endless process of rationalization, not through the production of linear, smooth, reassuring narratives that would offer a shelter from the randomness of fate, but through the streamlining of discourse in texts that undertake to integrate the lacunae and discrepancies of partial, selective, inventive memories.

This chapter proposes an analysis of Hejinian's landmark texts – "Happily", mostly, but also *Writing Is an Aid to Memory*, and the three instalments of *My Life* –, which I all read as being "always conscious of the disquieting runs of life slipping by, that the message remains undelivered, opposed to [us]" (*Writing Is an Aid*, "Preface"), It is all a matter of seeking better textual and narrative adequacy with the real conditions of life, with the reality of experiencing life "slipping by". *Slowly*, the sequel to "Happily", shifts the focus on adverbial strategies, which modulate the assertiveness of action, so that the accounts of precariousness become in themselves precarious, provisional and tentative. With *The Fatalist*, a collection of poems that follows "Happily" and *Slowly*, and is contemporary with some instalments of *My Life*, a form of acceptance and a resolve to live in the precariousness of what happens is turned into an existential philosophy. Based on both remembrance and projection, it seems therefore that Hejinian's poems attempt to capture the flitting duration of the present moment, the moment of composition and poetic actualization acting also as a testimony of this unsettling experience of the flitting and of the impossibility of definitive statements of facts.

Such assessments of personal history converge with Slavoj Žižek's suggestion that if we are not able to confront historical traumas, they will continue to haunt us, and that if we want to really forget an event, we have paradoxically to remember it (46). It is also by being able to remember that one can transmit one's experience: by remembering, narrativizing the traumatic event, be it personal or collective, one is able to recover from it, regain the balance that was once disrupted. In a more pessimistic, less positive or encouraging approach, however, the recovery may be endlessly postponed because the narrative is flawed, the remembrance fictitious, and the disorder the source of increasing estrangement or defamiliarization – by which I mean, along with Hejinian, Viktor Shklovsky's *ostranenie*. Hence the resistance to narrativization one finds in Hejinian's work. In this respect, she symptomatically fails to mention what triggered the writing of "Happily", and it was Marjorie Perloff, in her review of the poem, who lifted the veil to reveal that the poem had come in the wake of "a bout with cancer":

> What Hejinian doesn't say in 'A Common Sense' [a meditation on Gertrude Stein's *Stanzas in Meditation* which precedes 'Happily' in *The Language of Inquiry*] is that her meditation on happiness was triggered by a bout with cancer from which she had recently recovered. In one sense, then, *Happily* is her poetic response to reprieve, to the happiness the poet experiences in recognizing her reinsertion into a state of *happening*. (21-22)

What Perloff does not perceive, though, is that for Hejinian cancer *was* this "happening", the unexpected state, this irruption of the random into the otherwise bearable uncertainty of life: a traumatic experience *per se*, but also above all the occasion of an epiphanic realization that causality remains a narrative-induced delusion. By entitling her poem "Happily", Hejinian therefore summons the ironies of word formation and the potential revelations they hold, suddenly aware of the conflation of the current meaning of the word with its etymological underpinnings – from the Old Norse *happ*, chance, fortune (good or bad). The poem thus points to the radical impossibility of living on 'happily', or on the surface of 'happiness'. Indeed, the recovery cannot occur, and forgetting is not an option, so that what remains is the spectacle of floundering subjects failing to construct seamless narratives. Forever they begin again and keep outlining ever-shifting causal networks. In his parallel comments on Hejinian and Carla Harryman, Srikanth Reddy describes their common refusal to accept the alphabetical rules of "consequence" – those selfsame rules Diderot's "Jacques Le Fataliste" also rejected, and to which Hejinian pays homage in *The Fatalist*:

> Perpetual beginning is not the only way to foreclose the fatality of consequence; Harryman's heroine, like Hejinian, changes the subject of her utterance in the middle of things, constructing a nonlinear poetics – 'for she couldn't draw a line and felt the following of lines to be too confining a game' – which ultimately entails an entire *ethos* of digression as well. (64-65)

In *Writing Is an Aid to Memory*, Lyn Hejinian meditates on both the saving function of writing, as it re-orders and re-motivates the often inconsequent succession of one's life events, or of history, and on its counterfeiting side-effects: by imposing linearity and coherence onto the past, writing about the past recreates it and produces discourses about which she, along with the other Language poets, feels extremely diffident. Attributed to Romanticism, the trust in the truthfulness and objectivity of any narrative account cannot be maintained, even though the interest in the workings of memory persists, so that other methods of representing the recomposeition of the past need to be sought. In Stephanie Sandler's words about Hejinian and her Russian friend and collaborator Arkadii Dragomoshchenko, "[t]he Romantics' belief in the saving powers of memory and imagination is also treated with some suspicion, although a fascination with the workings of recollection and invention persists" (42).

Ever since Ron Silliman's essay about "the New Sentence", Hejinian and others have been walking a tightrope between Benveniste's interrogations about syntactic "integration" (Silliman, *In the American Tree*, 570) and Stein's assertions in her 1926 lecture "Composition as Explanation" about the emotion tucked in a paragraph (518-523). What is at stake is the production of what one might call the lowest level of meaning, one which would simultaneously produce meaning and preclude meaningfulness, thus confining the reader to the limbo of understanding as a permanent process, forever unable to reach a conclusion, the stability of a final statement. Indeed, the slips of grammar in Hejinian's texts prevent grammatical cohesion, and the disjunctive composition of her stanzas or paragraphs provides texts that remain shifting and adjusting, but never adjusted.

This is an example taken from *Writing Is an Aid to Memory*:

> Memory cannot, though the future return, and proffer raw confusions. Knowledge is part of the whole, as hope is, from which love seeks to contrast knowledge with separation, and certainty with the temporal. Abridgement is foolish, like a lopping off among miracles; yet times is not enough. Necessity is the limit with forgetfulness, but it remains undefined. Memory is the girth, or again. (n.p.)

One from "Happily":

> Constantly I write this happily
> Hazards that hope may break open my lips
> What I feel is taking place, a large context, long unyielding, and to doubt it would be a crime against it
> I sense that in stating 'this is happening'
> Waiting for us? (385)

And from the last sentences of *My Life in the Nineties*:

> The old woman 'seeks solitude', her mind 'is elsewhere', she 'loves to roam in the woods', she 'has visions', and she 'sings in her sleep'. We are not forgetting the patience of the mad, their love of detail (a cellist in a tree with a microscope and a badger in bed with a book, etc.) – everyone is out of place in a comedy. One must eliminate fear in order to create a space for living an ethical life. Subjectivity at night must survive hours during which it encounters nothing that is conscious of it and have nothing to judge but itself. (87-88)

In each of these instances, Hejinian's syntax proves extremely difficult to parse, when it does not entirely fail to stabilize. The process of reading becomes characterized by a to-and-fro movement, as the reader's gaze, along with her understanding, laboriously progresses forward after having given up on full comprehension and accepted incompleteness. Irredeemably failing to exhaust a topic, or to get to the core of the argument, the poem becomes the "girth" by which Hejinian defines memory: it circles, approximates, underscores in fact a void whose "abridgement" is vain. This oscillating movement Charles Bernstein analyzes in his essay about critical writing and the fusion of poetry and poetics:

> Poetry in its most ecstatic manifestation is a nonlinear dynamic system. The vortex that poetics spins is a bubbling desynchronization chamber. But poetic chaos, like the chaotic phenomena mapped by recent physics, is not absolute but constrained. It is controllable not in its flowering but in the progression toward chaos and the regression from it. We can study this progression into chaos, or move backward out of it: perhaps this is the narrative of a poem that poetics can address. (845)

In rejecting the closure brought about by apparent univocality, and in working out non-linear narrative modes, Hejinian "ejects [...] the idea that there is something containable to say: completed saying. So that poetics becomes an activity that is ongoing, that moves in different directions at the same time, and that tries to disrupt or make problematic any formulation that seems too final or preemptively restrictive" (Bernstein 830).

To this extent, the three instalments of *My Life* illustrate tactics of survival in the paradigmatic, meant to counter the commonplace survival in the delusions of fictitious coherence. The first two are based on a relatively simple procedure to generate the text of the poet's autobiography. The "new sentence", with its refusal of syntactic complexity, is the unit that composes the chapters of the autobiographical text. The fabric of the text constantly questions the relevance of a smooth rational narrative of one's past, as it is torn by disruptions, non-sequiturs, and lacunae. The text presents the snippets of memories as memory yields them, partial and disorganized, retrieved through association without the artifice of chronological or causal reorganization, and assembled in what Bernstein calls Hejinian's "modular style" (832). In each of the first two instalments (*My Life* at 37, and *My Life* at 45), the number of chapters corresponds to the poet's age (respectively 37 and 45), and the number of sentences in each chapter takes over this constraint so that each is respectively 37- or 45-sentence long. The second instalment, then, does function on the "modular" principle, since it is a reorganization of the entire biographical account that ensues from the poet's ageing. The memory of the first year is altered, recombined by the addition of years in the poet's whole life, in a process which is incremental and non-linear. Each year has its chapter, but it contains the number of sentences corresponding to the present of writing, so that each remembrance of the past is embossed with the poet's present age. The micro-changes from the first to the second instalment evidence the prismatic functioning of memory, irredeemably distorting what it feigns to retrieve and restore to consciousness:

> We see only the leaves and branches of the trees close in around the house. Those submissive games were sensual. I was no more than three or four years old, but when crossed *I would hold my breath not from rage but from stubbornness, until I lost consciousness.* The shadows one day deeper. Every family has its own collection of stories, but not every family has someone to tell them. In a small studio in an old farmhouse, it is the musical expression of a glowing optimism. A bird would reach but be secret. Absence of allusion:

> once, and ring alone. The downstairs telephone was in a little room as dark as a closet. *It made a difference between the immediate and the sudden in a theater filled with transitions. Without what can a person function as the sea functions without me.* A typical set of errands. (*My Life* 14 and *Lyn Hejinian Papers* MSS 74 Box 40 Folder 15)

As long as the poet will grow old, the project of *My Life* will increase, defying finitude – at least, this is the fiction which the poem weaves until the third and last instalment. For *My Life in the Nineties* picks up the general outlook of *My Life*, but the numbers do not cohere in the same manner. The poet is now in her fifties, she is therefore writing after "Happily", and each of the ten chapters contains fifty sentences, as if time had frozen over the decade of pain. The two former instalments are not worked back into the text, so that a caesura is performed, negating the "continuity" advertised on the back cover of the book. Where *My Life* is widely commented by critics, *My Life in the Nineties* remains elusive, an addition that does not add up, unless one is willing to recognize the radical failure of life to add up, even in the method of Hejinian's modular, combinatorial, incremental procedure. As the poem reaches us, as it resonates with the unsaid of "Happily", one is sent back to Hejinian's appraisal of happiness as "a complication of the ordinary", a "folding in of the happenstantial" ("A Common Sense" 371), and to Derrida's comment on the referential in Celan:

> Ces choses, qui ne sont pas seulement des mots, le poète est seul à pouvoir en témoigner mais il ne les nomme pas dans le poème. La possibilité du secret, en tout cas, reste toujours ouverte et cette réserve est inépuisable. (Derrida 12)

It is precisely by not narrating pain, disaster, despair, that the poet makes us catch a glimpse of the horror of the "atelic, goal-free, aimless" that shapes our lives, and for which there is no accounting – just a provisional discounting. If the subject is to survive, the "hazard of happiness" (*My Life in the Nineties* 57) must be explored over and over again, but it will not be controlled, just as life will not be programmed. The poetics and the politics intertwine to reclaim the very locus of existential uncertainty and "happily" conquer its indeterminacies:

> It is a writing of reasons. It is a politics, a chance. If we received our fate at birth, then the question one would have to ask of a child is how will she behave while she awaits her fate. (*My Life in the Nineties* 57-58)

Works Cited

Bernstein, Charles. "Optimism and Critical Excess (Progress)." *Critical Inquiry* 16:4 (1990): 830-856.

Derrida, Jacques. *Poétique et politique du témoignage*. Paris: L'Herne, 2005.

Diderot, Denis. *Jacques le Fataliste et son maître*. Paris: Laffont, 1994.

Hejinian, Lyn. "A Common Sense." *The Language of Inquiry*. Berkeley: The University of California Press, 2000. 355-382.

—. *The Fatalist*. Richmond: Omnidown, 2003.

—. "Happily." *The Language of Inquiry*. Berkeley: The University of California Press, 2000. 383-406.

—. *The Lyn Hejinian Papers*. New Poetry Archive, Mandeville Special Collections: University of California San Diego.

—. *My Life*. Los Angeles: Green Integer, 2002.

—. *My Life in the Nineties*. New York: Shark Books, 2003.

—. "The Rejection of Closure" [1983]. *The Language of Inquiry*. Berkeley: The University of California Press, 2000. 40-58.

—. *Slowly*. Berkeley: Tuumba Press, 2002.

—. *Writing Is an Aid to Memory*. 1978. Los Angeles: Sun & Moon, 1996.

Olson, Charles. "Projective Verse." *Collected Prose*. Ed. Donald Allen and Benjamin Friedlander. Berkeley: University of California Press, 1997. 239-249.

Perloff, Marjorie. "Happy World: What Lyn Hejinian's Poetry Tells Us about Chance, Fortune, and Pleasure." *Boston Review* 26.1 (2001): 21-22.

Reddy, Shrikanth. "Changing the Sjuzet: Lyn Hejinian's Digressive Narratologies." *Contemporary Literature* 50.1 (2009): 54-93.

Sandler, Stephanie. "Arkadii Dragomoshchenko, Lyn Hejinian, and the Persistence of Romanticism." *Contemporary Literature* 46.1 (2005): 18-45.

Shklovsky,Viktor. "Art as Technique." 1917. *Literary Theory: An Anthology*. Ed. Julie Rivkin and Michael Ryan. Malden, MA: Blackwell, 1998. 17-23.

Silliman, Ron. *In the American Tree*. Orono: National Poetry Foundation, 1986.

—. *The New Sentence*. New York: Roof, 1987.

Stein: Gertrude. *Selected Writings*. Ed. Carl Van Vechten. New York: Vintage, 1972.

Žižek, Slavoj. *Bienvenue dans le désert du réel*. Paris: Flammarion, 2007. [English Original: *Welcome to the Desert of the Real! Five Essays on September 11 and Related Dates*. London: Verso, 2002].

Elisabeth Angel-Perez

"I am the place of my wound": Precarious Lives on the Contemporary English Stage

1. Introduction

Precarious humanity, apprehended in its historical dimension or reflected at the level of the individual, has been the focal point of British theatre ever since World War II. The same theme has been a major theatrical preoccupation with an intensity that is slightly different but by no means weaker in the era of capitalist globalization. What is shown on the contemporary stage is the for-ever open wound: "I am the place of my wound" (159), Edward Bond writes in *The Hidden Plot*. The theatre of today's major dramatists is essentially a post-tragic theatre insofar as it refrains from instituting itself as a place of consensus and of restoration of order, aiming rather to expose the unhealed fractures and traumas of humanity and of the synecdochic subject, representative of the whole of mankind. The end of the twentieth century, marked by the prominence of "In-Yer-Face Theatre" (Sierz) itself pioneered by Edward Bond's dramaturgy of the "aggro-effects",[1] pushed the logic of explicit violence to its very limit. During the 'nasty 90s', frontal violence on the stage, known as the New Brutalist movement, was thriving, characterized in particular by the exhibition of the suffering body as a phenomenological approach to precariousness, the exposure of the suffering body as the visible sign of precarious lives.

Conversely, a number of contemporary plays have paradoxically developed an aesthetics which relies more on the 'voiced' than on the 'shown': this is the case of 'verbatim theatre', which uses the real words of interviewees,[2] or more particularly of such dramatists as Sarah Kane, Martin Crimp or, more recently, debbie tucker green, who do not show precarious lives on the stage, but narrate them, thus moving away from the dramatic, performed, dimension of theatre in favour of the epic, narrated one. As if aggressivity-based innovation were no longer possible, visual aggression as a dramatic mode has lost ground and the most efficient stage expositions of precarious lives either opt for narration, or have become performative self-vocalizations of the jeopardized subject, songs of my (lost) self, so to speak: "watch me vanish / watch me / watch /

[1] Edward Bond's "aggro-effect" or aggressivity-effect, a concept coined after Bertolt Brecht's alienation effect (A-Effect), aims at shocking the spectator awake through frontal aggression. The spectator is therefore not only intellectually alert but viscerally disturbed.

[2] David Hare is one of the leading voices of the verbatim theatre. His plays are either based on interviews (*The Permanent Way* (2003), a play about the privatization of the Railways in Britain, stages Passengers speaking the real words of the passengers they stand for) or on the public statements made by political personalities: Toni Blair, Condoleezza Rice or George Bush in *Stuff Happens* (2004).

Open the curtains" (Kane, *4:48* 42-43; final words). Performativity has shifted from the body, with its capacity to impersonate and to enact, to the language in its thanatographic enterprise, therefore paving the way for a drama of words and of voices. The precarious self as body is therefore elided, erased, crossed out, and yet revealed through its very physical absence, compelling the spectator to renegotiate the spectacular contract.

2. Spectralizing the Body: Epicizing Precariousness

Whereas the classic mode of theatre relies on the specular or the spectacular – the word 'theatre', as is well known, comes from the Greek word *thea*, meaning eyesight –, a number of recent plays have opted out of *opsis* and into *diegesis* to address the subject of the wounded or traumatic self. Some of these stage experiments have sometimes been conducted in the playful mode. This is what verbatim and mock-verbatim theatre dramatists have tried to do. Dennis Kelly's extremely disquieting mock-verbatim drama, *Taking Care of Baby* (2007), is a case in point.

This documentary-style play narrates the story of Donna, convicted for killing her two babies and interviewed by the playwright about her life in prison. The play shows Donna telling her story, highlighting the fact that this is based on the true life of Donna McAuliffe, imprisoned for murdering her children, a story that the audience would most probably have had in mind at the time the play was first performed. The performance begins with the explicit statement that "[t]he following has been taken word for word from interviews and correspondence. Nothing has been added and everything is in the subject's own words, though some editing has taken place" (3). The audience is therefore invited to look at the whole wretched spectacle of Donna telling about herself as if they were a collective camera eye and recording device. It is only after a while that, owing to a number of implausibilities, the audience begins to understand that this is indeed a mock-verbatim play, and that Kelly has been faking it: the words uttered on the stage are not Donna's, but only lent to her by the dramatist. Kelly's play thus implicitly questions the aesthetic exploitation of precariousness carried out in the media and on the stage, but also challenges the very notion of verbatim theatre as a genre, raising the question of the reliability of 'truth' whenever it is appropriated by the media.

Although developing an aesthetics at odds with the gravity of the themes dealt with, verbatim and mock-verbatim theatre can be regarded as highly genuine stage experiments which try to grasp the true bewilderment and angst of precarious selves. However, leaving aside the playfulness of the devices chosen by dramatists like Dennis Kelly or David Hare, my concern in this chapter will be with plays which engage in post-tragic aesthetics, and whose aim is to renovate and reconceptualize the genre of tragedy. The whole of Kane's work is concerned with expressing the precariousness of lives on the stage – those of cancer-devoured Ian and of anorexic Cate in *Blasted* (1995), that of grunger Hippolytus and suicidal Phaedra in *Phaedra's Love* (1996), that of hermaphrodites Grace and Graham in *Cleansed* (1998), and that of a choric unnamed lyrical subject in *Crave* (1998) and *4:48 Psychosis* (2000). But what best characterizes Kane's work is that it epitomizes an evolution from sheer frontality to the elision of monstration.

Indeed, Kane's poetics evolved from an aggressive visuality (*Blasted*) and over-exposure of the body to a spectralization of the body, which is made to progressively vanish in favour of voice. Like Beckett's dramatic work, which undergoes a progressive deconstruction from *Godot* to *Not I*, for example, or to the utmost radicality of *Breath*, Kane's plays can be described as following a funnel-shaped progression: *Blasted*, *Phaedra's Love* and *Cleansed* are crowded with characters and overbrimming with bodily presence onstage – diseases, sexual aggressions, the martyred body are constantly exhibited. Mid-way into Kane's deconstruction of this initial frame, *Crave* stages four characters whose names have been replaced by mere letters – A, B, C, M –, four almost interchangeable living-dead voices barking their pain to one another. Finally, *4:48 Psychosis* materializes the decomposition of character and, behind it, of subjecthood: there are no more letters, not even voices, Kane now using mere dashes to indicate the presence of a speaker, and sometimes no dashes at all, so that the reader does not even know if the line is actually meant to be spoken out, thus entailing a generic porosity between play and poetry. As the play jeopardizes the survival of the subject, it challenges the very concept of theatre as a place used for showing. Ultimately it questions the very necessity of a text meant to be spoken out on a stage. The characters retreat into the shadows, and voice alone keeps lamenting "a solo symphony" (*4:48* 40; final words) spoken by a Per-se-phone-like persona.

Whereas theatre aims at showing the life of people and things – ever since the age of Greek tragedy, to leave the stage has been experienced as metaphorical death –, in Kane's plays the traumatic subject enacts his or her own precariousness by being progressively erased, hollowed out of his/her presence. The word 'trauma' shares its Indo-European etymology with the French *trou*, meaning a 'hole'. And indeed, trauma punches holes in the surface of the visible, it wipes away. It is this spectralization of the subject that Kane's theatre invites us to attend 'live': first, by spectralizing the flesh and blood body, as we have seen; then, by spectralizing the body of the text, literally 'traumatizing' it. The wounds inflicted on the human body are made to ricochet off the body of language, and just as the flesh is martyred, language seems to be tortured. Asyntactic, deprived of punctuation, it serializes itself either through chopped up hyper-stichomythic exchanges – "C. The vision. / M. The loss. / C. The pain. / A. The loss. / B. The gain. / M. The loss. / C. The light" (*Crave* 40) – or through a cyclical form:

> flash flicker slash burn wring press dab slash
> flash flicker punch burn float flicker dab flicker
> punch flicker flash burn dab press wring press
> punch flicker float burn flash flicker burn (*4:48* 29)

As the body undergoes a process of distintegration, parataxis is made to replace syntax. In addition to dismantling the structure of the sentence, Kane drills holes in the words themselves, which are sometimes replaced by acronyms, such as QED, or RSVP ASAP (*Crave* 28; *4:48* 12). These are at first readable, before they eventually become illegible, as with MNO (*Crave* 32), sending us back to what is left of the alphabet, to a ruin of the word, or to some sort of archeo- or proto-word suggesting a 'before' of articulated language. Another logic, that of mathematics, seeks henceforth to take over:

100
93
86
79
72
65
58
51
44
37
30
23
16
9
2 (*4:48* 30)

From the all engulfing shroud-like silence that threatens to eat up the speaking voice – the last two pages of Kane's play feature a few choreographed words speaking out their own disappearance – to dagger-like words paratactically juxtaposed, the hole-digging affects the structure of the play, which presents itself as a succession of 24 sections – from the Latin *secare*, to cut – suggesting as many lacerations, its syntax, its lexis and finally down to its very letters being eventually replaced by numbers (cf. Angel-Perez, *Voyages*). Tortured language thus echoes bodily pain, but also expresses ontological suffering; the compulsive invasion of silence mimics death's invading protocol. Kane dramatizes the presence of a voice listening to its own entry into silence, produces self-elegies, songs of its lost self.

3. The Globalization of Precariousness

Martin Crimp's *Attempts on Her Life* (1997) takes us one step further in the process of narrativization and spectralization. The play, subtitled "17 scenarios for the theatre", is very much in the tradition of OuLiPian games, notably of the "Exercices de style" (i.e., exercises in style) practised by Raymond Queneau and Jean Tardieu. The spectator is shown seventeen failed attempts at getting hold of Anne, a character who, although central, never appears on the stage. Variously described as a terrorist, a movie star, a car (the new Anny), a TV set or a contemporary installation artist, the protean Anne is in fact missing, just as missing as reality which, in our postmodern world, is permanently hidden by the manifold layers of representations – "simulacra" as Baudrillard calls them – which keep us at a distance from hard facts. Like the missing 'e' of George Perec's lipogrammatic novel, *La Disparition* (*A Void*, trans. Gilbert Adair), Anne is never to be seen.

Crimp shows the obliteration of women's life in society, but more broadly speaking, and beyond the feminist reading of the play, with(out) Anne he gives us a metonymical and gendered representation of the globalized subject (cf. Zimmermann). The protagonist of a lipogrammatic or lipoprosopic play, i.e. a play whose main face has been absented (cf. Angel-Perez, "Language Games"), Anne is neither seen nor heard, but only re-membered in her precariousness by the voices of her kin or friends or enemies. This practice which consists in wiping out the characters' bodies while having their lives taken over by the voices of others, defines is characteristic of a postmodern ethics: the decentered voice favours the expression of a nomadic subject, a 'dis-identitied' subject whose precariousness paradoxically enable him/her to avoid being trapped in any kind of determinism, be it of gender, social class or age.

If Crimp and his 'rememb(e)rers' blur the sexual and social frontiers of identity and do away with the essentialism of voice, British-Jamaican playwright debbie tucker green – her refusal of hierarchy accounting for the spelling of her name without capital letters – definitely crosses the frontiers and exposes the emergence of a globalized, post-national precarious subject. In *Stoning Mary*, she intertwines three stories of precariousness – dealing with the stoning of women, the issue of child soldiers and the problems related to the cost of treating AIDS (only one prescription for two patients) – which seem to be situated in non-European countries. Indeed, the situation of a woman about to be stoned sounds cruelly exotic, the characters' diction is ethnically marked, its rhythm technically close to rap or slam:

> OLDER SISTER You spectin some stay of exe-somethin?
> YOUNGER SISTER Got no stay of exe-fuckin-nuthin have I.
> … Not even the women. Not even the women?
> OLDER SISTER … No.
> YOUNGER SISTER So what happened to the womanist bitches
> … the feminist bitches?
> …The professional bitches.
> What happened to them?
> What about the burn their bra bitches?
> The black bitches
> The rootsical bitches … (60)

Still more radically, *Random* (2008) narrates the day when a black teenager leaves his home and gets killed by the police. The list of dramatis personae states the presence of Mum, Sister and Brother onstage, yet paradoxically indicates that the roles should be played by a single actress ("one black actress plays all the characters") developing a long monologue in the mode of hypotyposis:

> So I —
> Give it my back —
> Roll on my front —
> Flex under the duvet —
> An lie there on the reluctant to get up —
> A rubbish night's sleep
> A restless night's sleep
> For no reason at all.
> Birds bitchin their birdsong outside.
> People already on road.

> Dogs in their yards barkin the shit outta
> The neighbourhood. (3-4)

The text is therefore delivered by an actress who speaks all the parts, but whose physical presence contradicts the very principle of voice delegation and double enunciation characteristic of drama. The play thus exposes what could be identified as a temptation of theatre, and then recoils from it. It is as if the play had been conceived so as to be spoken by various characters – granted an interior life of their own – who would however never be allowed to enjoy an onstage existence. The textual regime is that of free indirect speech, but somehow it is homogenized by a vicarious empathic enunciator.

This is reminiscent of the technique perfected by Virginia Woolf in her own version of the stream of consciousness, that of the homogeneous unifying voice in *Mrs Dalloway,* where the interior monologue is spoken out by the voice of a figure comparable to that of a narrator allowing the protagonist into existence. In *Random*, the character is not only deprived of a body, but also of his/her own voice, in a gesture that confirms the exile of the subject from him/herself on the post-Beckettian stage. The interior monologue, as Jean-Pierre Sarrazac has pointed out, is no longer the privilege of the novel (130); on the contemporary stage, however, it stands out as a curiously paradoxical device, since it arises from an often-absent and always-silent body.

4. A Theatre of Obliteration

The paradox is that the more absent the body of the character, the more intrusive it becomes; the more amputated or erased, the more present. The trauma makes holes in the substance of the body, ends up eradicating it from the visible world, and yet in doing so reveals it. Voice, the only corporeal witness left of the martyred body – and one should bear in mind that etymologically 'martyr' means 'witness' – constitutes not so much a prosthetic body as a "meta-body" (Cohen-Levinas 41), which speaks a body that it also simultaneously spectralizes. This brings us very close to Levinas's art of "obliteration", a concept that the philosopher develops to analyze the work of Sacha Sosno, a French sculptor whose method consists in either cutting out the inside of his works or in denying them the possibility of a completed form. The concept of obliteration captures the oxymoronic quality of such sculptures, which give and withdraw at the same time, at once creating and denying form.

Sarah Kane, Martin Crimp or debbie tucker green's procedures of "obliteration" are very much in the continuation of Beckett's theatre of hollowness. Although each in his or her own manner, the three of them build a paradoxical system which consists first in tearing an image from the night – recalcitrance and reluctance are the very condition of any image, for "if the image didn't refuse itself to us, the work would have no justification" (Savinel 156) – only to plunge it back into night. At a political and ethical level, Levinas would probably argue that this paradoxical presence/absence of the form is also a way of denying the spectator the enjoyment of visual pleasure, of depriving him or her of the possibility of being totally seduced by art, so that the sufferings of the world can become perceptible again: "The perfection of the beautiful imposes silence regardless of the rest. It is the guardian of silence. It lets things happen. This is where aesthetic civilisation has its limits [...] art makes one insensitive to the sufferings of the world" (Levinas 8; my translation). What I call the 'theatre of obliteration' designed by dramatists such as Kane, Crimp or green both gives and takes. It narrates what it cannot show, and therefore denies the thing any material visibility while allowing it a vocal and literary coming into shape. The traumatic subject is therefore summoned on stage through an art which respects the very nature of trauma in its inexpressibility. This dramatic treatment of the precarious subject can thus be seen as a clever way to by-pass a couple of aesthetic aporias: the impossibility of showing that which shuns coming to light – the trauma; but also the ethical dead end of an art which may paralyze thought by offering it the spectacle of the beautiful or of perfection. The art of obliteration, which might also be called the art of "crossing out" ("barrer" (29), Levinas says in French), brings to light the drama of being, exposes the wound of being, neither wholly abdicating its right to aesthetic enjoyment nor allowing itself to drift into an aestheticization of suffering or voyeurism – notwithstanding the inevitable operation of mimesis which turns the unacceptable into a source of pleasure or into an aesthetic feeling if only because of the technical feasibility of representing violence or pain. With such innovative dramaturgies, the theatre effectively finds a way to represent the inexpressible or the traumatic. Precariousness condemns the subject to invisibility, and yet invisibility, when it is framed and displayed as an object for the gaze, reveals more than the visible itself.

Works Cited

Angel-Perez, Elisabeth. "Language Games and Literary Constraints: Playing with Tragedy in the Theatre of Caryl Churchill and Martin Crimp." *Contemporary British Theatre: Breaking New Ground*. Ed. by Vicky Angelaki. London: Palgrave Macmillan, 2013. 79-95.

—. *Voyages au bout du possible: Les théâtres du traumatisme de Samuel Beckett à Sarah Kane*. Paris: Klincksieck, 2006.

Baudrillard, Jean. *Simulacres et simulations*. Paris: Galilée, 1980.

Beckett, Samuel. *Complete Dramatic Works*. London: Faber, 1986.

Bond, Edward. *The Hidden Plot*. London: Methuen, 2000.

Cohen-Levinas, Danielle. *La Voix au-delà du chant - Une fenêtre aux ombres*. Paris: Vrin, 2006.

Crimp, Martin. *Attempts on Her Life*. London: Faber, 1997.

Kane, Sarah. *Blasted*. London: Methuen, 1995.

—. *Cleansed*. London: Methuen, 1998.

—. *Crave*. London: Methuen, 1998.

—. *Phaedra's Love*. London: Methuen, 1996.

—. *4:48 Psychosis*. London: Methuen, 2000.

Kelly, Dennis. *Taking Care of Baby*. 2007. London: Oberon, 2012.

Levinas, Emmanuel. *De l'oblitération: à propos de Sosno*. Paris: La Découverte, 1990.

Sarrazac, Jean-Pierre. *L'Avenir du drame*. Saulxures: Circé, 1999.

Savinel, Christine. "De la résistance comme un visage." *L'Ombre de l'image, de la falsification à l'infigurable*. Ed. Muriel Gagnebin. Seyssel: Champ Vallon, 2002.

Sierz, Aleks. *In-Yer-Face Theatre*. London: Faber, 2001.

tucker green, debbie. *Random*. London: Nick Hern, 2008.

—. *Stoning Mary*. London: Nick Hern, 2005.

Zimmermann, Heiner. "Images of Woman in Martin Crimp's *Attempts on Her Life*." *European Journal of English Studies* 7.1 (2003): 69-85.

Index

The Contributors

Hélène Aji is professor of American literature at the Université de Paris Ouest Nanterre. In addition to a number of articles on Modernist and contemporary American poetry as well as books on Pound, Williams and Ford, she recently edited an issue of the *Revue Française d'Études Américaines* on the discourses of truth in literature and history (2013).

Marc Amfreville is professor of American literature at Université Paris IV-Sorbonne. He is co-author of *Histoire de la littérature américaine* (2010) and works on representations of trauma in North-American fiction, among other topics.

Elisabeth Angel-Perez is professor of English literature at Université Paris IV-Sorbonne. She specialises in British theatre and drama of the twentieth and twenty-first centuries and has also translated numerous plays into French.

Ellen Dengel-Janic is a lecturer in English literature and cultural studies at the University of Tübingen. Her major interests are in the field of postcolonial and gender studies, and Indian literature in English and South Asian diasporic culture.

Rudolph Glitz is a lecturer of English literature at the University of Amsterdam. He has written on nineteenth and early twentieth-century fiction as well as popular culture. A long-term research interest of his is in literary constructions of generational and age-group identities.

Stephanie Hoppeler is a PhD student at the University of Berne. She is engaged in a larger research project on graphic novels.

Barbara Kowalczuk is affiliated with Université Montesquieu Bordeaux IV. Her research interests lie in literary and photographic representations of war and trauma.

Barbara Korte is professor of English literature at the University of Freiburg. Her research areas include travel writing, the literature of World War I and the literary representation of poverty.

Stephan Laqué is a lecturer at Ludwig Maximilians University, Munich. His research interests include early modern literature, modernism and postmodernism, as well as literary and cultural theory.

Jagna Oltarzewska lectures in the Department of English and American Studies at the University of Paris IV-Sorbonne. She has published on contemporary North American authors and her research interests also include literary theory and intercultural translation.

Frédéric Regard is professor of English literature at the Sorbonne in Paris. He has written several books and articles on nineteenth and twentieth-century authors and has edited collections of essays on life-writing, exploration narratives and early Arctic voyages.

Gabriele Rippl is professor and chair of Literatures in English at the University of Berne. Her publications focus on North American and British literature and culture, with a special interest in the interplay of different symbolic systems.

Lena Steveker is a lecturer at the University of Saarland, Saarbrücken. She specialises in contemporary British fiction, popular culture and early-modern literature. Her current interest is the interaction of theatre and news culture in early-modern England.